YES, BUT NOT QUITE

YES, BUT NOT QUITE

*Encountering Josiah Royce's
Ethico-Religious Insight*

DWAYNE A. TUNSTALL

FORDHAM UNIVERSITY PRESS   NEW YORK   2009

Copyright © 2009 Fordham University Press

All rights reserved. No part of this publication may be reproduced, stored in a retrieval system, or transmitted in any form or by any means—electronic, mechanical, photocopy, recording, or any other—except for brief quotations in printed reviews, without the prior permission of the publisher.

Fordham University Press has no responsibility for the persistence or accuracy of URLs for external or third-party Internet websites referred to in this publication and does not guarantee that any content on such websites is, or will remain, accurate or appropriate.

Library of Congress Cataloging-in-Publication Data
Tunstall, Dwayne A.
 Yes, but not quite : encountering Josiah Royce's ethico-religious insight / Dwayne A. Tunstall. — 1st ed.
  p. cm.
 Includes bibliographical references and index.
 ISBN 978-0-8232-3054-9 (cloth : alk. paper)
 1. Royce, Josiah, 1855–1916. 2. Idealism. 3. Personalism. 4. Ethics. 5. Religion. 6. Metaphysics. 7. Howison, George Holmes, 1834–1917. I. Title.
  B945.R64T86 2009
  191—dc22   2008047151

Printed in the United States of America
11 10 09   5 4 3 2 1
First edition

For Crystal

"Lovin' you whether, whether/ Times are good or bad, happy or sad"
—Al Green, "Let's Stay Together"

Contents

Preface ix
Acknowledgments xiii

    Introduction: Encountering Josiah Royce's
    Ethico-Religious Insight   1

PART I. JOSIAH ROYCE'S PERSONALISM

1. The "Conception of God" Debate:
   Setting the Stage for Royce's Personalism   9

2. Haunted by Howison's Criticism:
   The Birth of Royce's Late Philosophy   28

3. Royce's Late Philosophy   51

4. Royce's Personalism   67

PART II. EXTENDING ROYCE'S ETHICO-RELIGIOUS INSIGHT: ROYCE ON THE BELOVED COMMUNITY, *AGAPE*, AND HUMAN TEMPORALITY

5. Royce's Ethico-Religious Insight:
   A Hypothetical Postulate?   85

6. King's Beloved Community, Royce's Metaphysics   96

7. Coupling Royce's Temporalism with Levinasian Insights   110

Closing Remarks   131

Notes   137
Bibliography   171
Index   181

Preface

This book began its life as my master's thesis at Southern Illinois University Carbondale, entitled "Josiah Royce's Personalism." To appreciate how all the diverse threads of philosophic argumentation in this book hang together, one must see how I initially conceived of the topic that became my master's thesis. I first imagined the topic for the thesis as I journeyed back to Carbondale, Illinois, from my parents' home in rural Tidewater Virginia, near the town of Tappahannock, during the 2002 Thanksgiving weekend. As I drove on U.S. Interstate 64 through eastern Kentucky, twenty miles or so from Moorehead, Kentucky, I listened to Michael Jackson's album *History*. On this album, there is this particularly heartfelt, depressing, and emotional song entitled "Little Susie." Jackson sings about a girl whose life appears to have been lived in vain. This song has always unnerved me somehow. At that moment, though, as I listened to it, I uncovered why this song had that effect on me. Shouldn't somebody remember the life of a little girl who loved, played, danced, cried, feared, suffered, dreamed, imagined, and desired? Who remembers *her*? In Jackson's song, only her neighbor remembered little Susie, but he did not really know her. She was only, at best, a tragic figure to him, not a dignified and wonderfully unique person whose life had (and still has) meaning and purpose.

Then, an answer to that question came to me as I drove in the night, surrounded by darkness: *God remembers her even when nobody else does!* But what does it mean to say that God remembers little Susie, or anyone else for that matter? I dedicated myself to fleshing

{ *ix* }

out the implications of that statement: *God remembers her even when nobody else does.* This task led me to read Josiah Royce's works, especially the religious and ethical works he wrote during the last years of his life. Indeed, Royce's later thought gave me the conceptual tools to work out some of the more technical implications of the statement that had inspired my inquiry. However, the more I read Royce's earlier works, the more I realized that Royce's entire philosophy was an extended answer to my initial question concerning Susie. Indeed, the entire first part of this book is the result of my initial meditations on "Little Susie."

As I wrote what eventually became part one of this book, I discovered that a fruitful way of approaching Royce's thought was to read Royce as an American personalist whose philosophy revolved around an ethico-religious insight. I interpret Royce's ethico-religious insight as one in which we are seen as participants in the divine life, but insofar as we live out the divine's eternal purpose in our own unique way. Frank Oppenheim, S.J., describes Royce's ethico-religious insight in these terms:

> [The divine] is viewed as a superhuman personal Subject, different from each finite self, yet being the ultimate center of identification for each self since the latter regards the Infinite Alter Ego as its own Other Self. . . . [T]his relationship to the Infinite Alter Ego runs through the whole human community as a . . . nonindividual, shared life that mediates between every member and the Infinite Alter Ego.[1]

After nearly two years of interpreting Royce's philosophy as a sort of personalism, I entered the twilight of my intellectual love affair with Royce's thought. Over the next year or so, I became more and more critical of Royce's absolutistic idealism.[2] Yet, amid my mounting criticism of Royce's absolutistic idealism, I remained convinced that Royce got something right in the formulation of his ethico-religious insight. In my subsequent writings about Royce's philosophy, I have attempted to conserve his ethico-religious insight while critiquing his rationalism and absolutism.

With this in mind, I should inform the reader that I wrote the sixth chapter on Royce and the Rev. Dr. Martin Luther King, Jr.'s conceptions of *agape* and the Beloved Community before my critical turn. The seventh chapter was written at the dawn of this critical turn in my analysis of Royce's philosophy; the Levinasian critique of Royce's ethical temporalism foreshadows my turn away from Royce's absolutistic idealism, and toward a more hospitable environment for his ethico-religious insight.[3] The fifth chapter was written after my critical turn and is a response to the recent interpretation of Royce's philosophy advanced by my friend and mentor Randall E. Auxier.

While Auxier reads Royce's philosophy as an interrelated series of hypothetical postulates whose meaningfulness is ultimately determined by their ethical import in our lives, I still yearn to read Royce's philosophy as one in which he advances philosophic propositions that actually describe some features of the world, as experienced by human persons, which substantiate his ethico-religious insight. I cling to this yearning despite the fact that I think that one can plausibly interpret Royce's philosophy in the way that Auxier does. Otherwise, I am not sure that anyone should spend time reading Royce beyond his later, fully developed ethics, because one could read, for example, William Ernest Hocking for the communitarian and religious dimensions of Royce's thought. Indeed, one would learn more from reading Hocking's insights on the nature of religious and secular communities than from reading Royce as a hypothetical metaphysician. As for logic and epistemology, I would prefer reading Charles Sanders Peirce over Royce. In that sense, I would agree with those Peirce scholars who judge Peirce to be a better logician and epistemologist than Royce.

However, when one reads Royce as a philosopher whose thought is founded on and sustained by a profound ethico-religious insight, he is worth reading as a metaphysician, and not only as an ethicist. Of course, this position on Royce's philosophy is considered outdated by a large number of American philosophers, including a large number of those philosophers who frequent the Society for the Advancement of American Philosophy. Nevertheless, I still seek to preserve the importance of Royce's ethico-religious insight despite the fact that his philosophic method cannot adequately account for it and that his religious thought is outside the philosophical mainstream.

As one reads this book, one should remember that it is a concise reevaluation of Royce's thought from the vantage point of his ethico-religious insight. It aims to describe Royce's ethico-religious insight as he might have done himself if he had self-consciously written in the philosophic language of American personalism. On a more personal level, what one will read in the following pages is how I encountered Royce's ethico-religious insight over a four-year time span. I hope that this discussion about my encounter with Royce's ethico-religious insight will motivate others to consider this insight as well.

Acknowledgments

If I had followed the conventions of academic philosophy, this book would not exist. Who would advise a second-year graduate student to revise and expand his master's thesis and submit it to a university press? My thesis committee—Randall E. Auxier, Kenneth W. Stikkers, and Stephen Tyman—did just that. I thank them for giving me the confidence to revise and expand that study, which led me to work for over three years to create this book. I especially thank my advisor, mentor, and friend, Randall E. Auxier, for the years of conversation on Josiah Royce and American philosophy that helped birth this book. I also thank Helen Tartar for taking a third-year graduate student seriously when he submitted a book proposal on Josiah Royce's ethico-religious insight and ensuring that it got a fair hearing. In addition, I would like to thank my fellow Royce scholars for encouraging me to write this book, especially Kim Garcher, Celia Bardwell-Jones, Jason Bell, Jackie Kegley, and Kelly Parker. Furthermore, I would like to thank my colleagues in the Philosophy Department at Grand Valley State University for providing me with a welcoming environment during the last stages of revising and editing this book. I would be remiss if I neglected to thank Eric Newman, managing editor of Fordham University Press, and Mary Christian, my copy editor, for their expert advice on how to improve this book. Heeding their advice has made this book much better than it would have been otherwise.

Because I am more than just an academic philosopher, I would like to thank those teachers and staff from Essex High School to Christopher Newport University who inspired me to pursue "the life of the mind," as Cornel West puts it. You know who you are.

During my graduate studies, I met many wonderful and talented academic philosophers-in-training who occasionally offered words of encouragement, a sympathetic ear, and even some memorable arguments. Of those I met, I would like to express my heartfelt gratitude to Dwight Welch, Tommy Curry, Tanya Jeffcoat, Bruce Buchanan, and Jason Hill. I could not ask for better friends and intellectual interlocutors than these. To those college friends I have lost contact with over the years, I appreciate the time I spent with each one of you. Whether we lost touch because of a tragic misunderstanding or a failure to communicate regularly with one another, I have not forgotten about you and what you mean to me. The same goes for those secondary and grade school friends whom I have lost contact with over the years.

I also would like to thank the students whom I taught at Grand Valley State University during the fall 2007 semester. It was thanks to them that I was able to think of a suitable title for this book. Originally, the title was supposed to be just, *Encountering Josiah Royce's Ethico-Religious Insight*. However, I was dissatisfied with that title; it sounded too academic, too bland. One of the manuscript reviewers felt the same way I did. For several months I searched for a suitable title. During that time, I graded more than 900 paper assignments. Over the course of grading those assignments, I had gotten into the routine of writing the phrase "not quite" in the margins beside those parts of the paper where I thought that a student did not quite understand a certain position. I realized that this is the way I feel about Royce most of the time when I read his writings about God. Despite the fact that I think Royce's ethico-religious insight is perhaps one of the best available modern descriptions of God, I cannot shake the feeling that Royce himself could never quite transcend his (overly) conceptual descriptions of God and let his readers intuit the God he describes: God the cosmic fellow-sufferer and God the loving Interpreter-Spirit. What better way to voice my thoughts on his ethico-religious insight than to entitle this book, *Yes, But Not Quite: Encountering Josiah Royce's Ethico-Religious Insight*?

Most important, I thank my wife, Crystal; my sons, Anthony and Christopher; my mother; my nieces and nephews; Anthony's maternal relatives; and my goddaughter, Destiny, for supporting me during the long writing process. They have collectively paid a debt that I can never repay.

Let me conclude by thanking Indiana University Press for its permission to revise and republish several lengthy passages from my article, "Concerning the God That Is Only a Concept: A Marcellian Critique of Royce's God," *Transactions of the Charles S. Peirce Society: A Quarterly Journal in American Philosophy* 42.3 (Summer 2006): 394–416, in the fifth chapter of this book.

YES, BUT NOT QUITE

INTRODUCTION

ENCOUNTERING JOSIAH ROYCE'S ETHICO-RELIGIOUS INSIGHT

Literature often bears to philosophy in general, and yet oftener to Ethical Philosophy, the relation of fountain to stream. What the poet suggests about the meaning and the obscurity of life, the ethical philosopher makes the subject of a formal study. The poet sees a tragedy of destiny; and the philosopher makes of it a problem in dialectics, where words war instead of souls. Certainly the stream in this case rises no higher than the source. No ethical system, unless it be the work of a philosopher who is himself a poet, will be found to have in it more insight into life than poetry has already suggested.

—Josiah Royce[1]

While this book neither mentions nor examines Josiah Royce's philosophy of literature and literary criticism, I begin this introduction with an epigram that characterizes Royce's general philosophical temperament. Royce is a poet-philosopher in the sense of being a philosopher who carefully hones words to communicate truths about the world, some of which transcend the boundaries of discursive thought. Like poetry, Royce's philosophy, at its best, dances on the fringe of ineffability, for example, when he discusses loyalty to loyalty in *The Philosophy of Loyalty* (1908), eternity in *The Sources of Religious Insight* (1912), and the Christian notions of grace and the Beloved Community in *The Problem of Christianity* (1913). From the essays on English literature, epistemology, and ethics he wrote while teaching English at the University of California, Berkeley[2] to his last manuscript, written only several hours before his death,[3] Royce tries to make the ineffable intelligible, to make himself and his reader more sensitive to the deafening whisper of the divine, telling us about the Beloved Community.

Inspired by the poetic undertones of Royce's writings, I consider this book to be an extended dialectical poem, using words, concepts, and arguments to articulate, criticize, and defend Royce's central insight—that is, Royce's insight that we are most alive and living up to our fullest potential when we commune with the Logos-Spirit and interact with one another in accordance with it. Father Frank M. Oppenheim calls this central insight Royce's "ethico-religious insight" in his several books on Royce's philosophy and intellectual development: *Royce's Voyage Down Under* (1980), *Royce's Mature Philosophy of Religion* (1987), *Royce's Mature Ethics* (1993), and *Reverence for the Relations of Life: Re-imagining Pragmatism via Josiah Royce's Interactions with Peirce, James, and Dewey* (2005).

In fact, this ethico-religious insight is at the heart of Royce's entire philosophy. He centers his philosophical thought on a metaphysics of community, on a metaphysics as old as the Judeo-Christian tradition but as recent as the late nineteenth century. Indeed, Royce's philosophy is a philosophical testament to Pauline Christianity and its emphasis on the Body of Christ as a universal agapic community. As early as Royce's 1896 essay "The Problem of Job," Royce's sympathies with Pauline Christianity are evident. Compare his notion of God as fellow-sufferer in "The Problem of Job," which I will discuss in more detail in Chapter 2, with St. Paul's comments in 1 Corinthians 12:25–26: "there should [ideally] be no schism in the body, but that the members should have the same care for one another. And if one member suffers, all the members suffer with it, or if one member is honored, all the members rejoice with it."[4]

One way to describe Royce's entire philosophical career is to say that he updates Paul's portrayal of the Body of Christ, of the community of persons, by redescribing the Judeo-Christian conception of God, first in post-Kantian terminology and, second, in Peircean terminology, especially Peirce's notion of evolutionary love. For Royce, this love is what holds the universe together; it is immanent in every temporal span and recognizable by finite-minded beings as the universe's overarching purpose. As such, these minded beings, sensing the desirability of pursuing more inclusive communities of persons and responding to the eternal nightingale's call for a more moral universe, are compelled by the divine allure of the ideal of the Beloved Community, and act to actualize the Beloved Community more and more in their daily encounters with other persons and non-minded beings alike.

Unlike many of the contemporary essays, articles, and books on Royce's philosophy,[5] this work affirms the religiosity of Royce's thought instead of trying to reformulate Royce's thought in secular terms. This is not to say that these contemporary writings about Royce's philosophy are antireligious or nonreligious; indeed, several of them are explicitly religious, especially if we accept John Dewey's notions of the religious (i.e., natural piety) and religious experience in *A Common Faith*.[6] All I am saying is that most of the portrayals of Royce's philosophy within contemporary American philosophical circles—especially among philosophers who participate in the Society for the Advancement of American Philosophy—are focused on interpreting his ethico-religious insight in secular terms.

Furthermore, only rarely do contemporary Royce scholars see him as an American personalist. This is very different than it was during the first couple of generations after Royce's death. For many philosophers of that time period, for example Edgar S. Brightman and W. H. Werkmeister, it was not unusual to associate Royce's philosophy with American personalism. I intend for this book to serve as a corrective to this unfortunate tendency in contemporary Royce scholarship. Indeed, I hope to demonstrate in this book that Royce's idealism is a type of American personalism—one which was directly challenged by George Holmes Howison's personal idealism—yet was more similar to Howison's personal idealism than either philosopher admitted during his lifetime, and one that has even more similarities to Boston personalist tradition than it does to Howison's personal idealism.

I have organized the chapters of *Yes, But Not Quite* into two parts. Part I (Chapters 1 through 4), "Josiah Royce's Personalism," situates

Royce's ethico-religious insight firmly within the American personalist tradition. It does so by documenting the development of Royce's ethico-religious insight in his initial reply and his subsequent, indirect replies to George Holmes Howison's criticism of his philosophy in their 1895 "Conception of God" debate at the University of California, Berkeley. These replies range from Royce's 1895 "Conception of God" lecture to Royce's *1915–16 Extension Course on Ethics*—all of which attempt to answer Howison's critical question to Royce: "How could any monistic idealism affirm the genuine moral agency of human persons if we are part of and dependent on the absolute for our very existence?" Once the development of Royce's ethico-religious insight in his thought is documented, I list the similarities and differences between his personalism and Howison's personal idealism. Then I compare Royce's personalism to Boston personalism, which I argue it is closer to than Howison's personal idealism.

Chapter 1 gives a brief history of the Royce-Howison debate in 1895 and reconstructs Howison's critiques of Royce's mostly epistemic arguments for God's existence, as Royce articulated them in *The Religious Aspect of Philosophy* (1885). It also analyzes Royce's modified ontological argument for God's existence in his 1895 lecture "The Conception of God." Additionally, it describes how Howison's criticism is a valid one, even though he misinterprets Royce's idealism and its argument for God's existence.

Chapter 2 documents and examines the development of Royce's ethico-religious insight in many of his writings, ranging from his 1896 essay "The Problem of Job" to *The Philosophy of Loyalty*. Chapter 3 continues the interpretative task by examining the significance of Royce's ethico-religious insight in his *The Problem of Christianity* and his *1915–16 Extension Course on Ethics*. I end this chapter with a comparison of Royce's personalism and Howison's personal idealism.

Chapter 4 describes how Royce's personalism fits within the American personalist tradition. Here I argue that Royce's personalism is more similar to Boston personalism than Howison's. To do this I analyze Royce's personalism in light of Rufus Burrow, Jr.'s account of Boston personalism in his *Personalism: A Critical Introduction*.[7] I end this chapter with a discussion of the continued significance of a Roycean personalism in today's intellectual climate.

Part II (Chapters 5 through 7), "Extending Royce's Ethico-Religious Insight: Royce on the Beloved Community, *Agape*, and Human Temporality," discusses Royce's ethico-religious insight in relation to Randall E. Auxier's interpretation of Royce's philosophy and two twentieth-century ethico-religious philosophers: King and Emmanuel Levinas. Chapter 5 is my attempt to confront the possibility that my reading of Royce is a mistaken one in light of Auxier's innovative interpretation of Royce's thought as advancing a fictional ontology, not an adequate description of reality. Chapter 6 compares King's philosophical theology, specifically his notions of the beloved community and *agape*, with Josiah Royce's metaphysics of community and its notion of the beloved community. In the process, I suggest how King's personalism, specifically his notion of the beloved community, could be strengthened by placing these notions in a Roycean metaphysical framework. I also suggest how King's philosophical nonviolence could serve as a more fertile ground for Royce's ethics and metaphysics of community than Royce's own later social and political positions, specifically his pro–World War I stance.

Chapter 7 considers how Royce could make the ethico-religious dimension of his temporalism explicit by incorporating certain insights from Levinas's phenomenology. Since most philosophers usually do not regard Royce as a temporalist philosopher, I dedicate an entire section to outlining Royce's temporalism, as articulated in the second volume of *The World and the Individual* and his 1910 essay "The Reality of the Temporal." Then I offer an all-too-concise description of Levinas's phenomenology of the face, his ethical metaphysics, and his temporalism in order to explain Levinas's temporalism, thus setting the stage for a Levinasian critique of Royce's temporalism. Then I subject Royce's temporalism to a Levinasian critique. Finally, I provide a brief outline of how the ethical import of Royce's temporalism might be strengthened once it incorporates certain Levinasian insights.

I conclude this book by briefly exploring the possibility that Royce's progressive racial anti-essentialism is, in fact, a form of cultural, anti-black racism and wonder if this taints his ethico-religious insight.

Given the apparent hodgepodge of philosophical topics, methods of argumentation, and exegesis gathered together into this single work, what single thesis or set of theses suffices to express them as a single philosophical project? This work contends that Royce bequeathed to the international philosophical community in general, and the American philosophical tradition in particular, a novel idealism based on an awe-inspiring ethico-religious insight—an idealistic personalism wherein the real is the personal and a metaphysics of community is the most appropriate approach to metaphysics for personal beings, especially in an often-impersonal and technological intellectual climate. I substantiate this by constructing a Roycean response to the criticisms of his idealism by George Holmes Howison and by reinterpreting Royce's idealism as an ethical and panentheistic personalism. Then, I confront the possibility that my reading of Royce is a mistaken one in light of Auxier's innovative interpretation of Royce's thought as advancing a fictional ontology, not an adequate description of reality. Once I explain why my reading of Royce is still a plausible one, despite the possibility that Royce did advance a fictional ontology, I examine how Royce's ethico-religious insight could be strengthened by incorporating the strengths of King's philosophical theology and of Levinas's phenomenology. I end with the suggestion that Royce's racial anti-essentialism is, in fact, a form of cultural, anti-black racism and question whether his anti-black racism taints his ethico-religious insight.

PART ONE

JOSIAH ROYCE'S PERSONALISM

ONE

THE "CONCEPTION OF GOD" DEBATE
Setting the Stage for Royce's Personalism

This book advances a thesis that is contrary to the majority opinion in Royce scholarship: I hold that Royce's late metaphysics of community[1] is not an extension of Royce's epistemological and logical concerns but rather an articulation of a living ethico-religious insight, an insight that serves as the animating force behind his entire philosophy.[2] Even Royce's earliest philosophical treatise, *The Religious Aspect of Philosophy* (1885), and its central argument for the existence of an Absolute Thought was not primarily an epistemological or a metaphysical defense of the Absolute's ontological status as the most real being in existence, but his initial attempt to describe the Absolute as a living *logos* that unites persons with each other, with every other finite being, and with the Absolute, while preserving their individuality.

That is, the apparently absolutist metaphysics of Royce's early philosophical career—spanning from his rejection of epistemic skepticism and acceptance of reality as a "divine Whole" guided by the

"World-Spirit," who serves as an omniscient, omni-benevolent person that we yearn to commune with, as the essential component of his philosophy in 1883[3] to the publication of *The Conception of God* (1895)—is his early attempt to delineate a metaphysics of community, of describing the mutual interdependence between the Absolute and finite individuals without reducing the latter to being simply modes of the Absolute manifesting himself,[4] temporally. I say "apparently absolutist metaphysics" here because Josiah Royce's Absolute never was a Hegelian Absolute, where the Absolute was the only real Individual. Royce always thought of the Absolute as the preserver of all particularities who lets them retain their ontological uniqueness. For Royce the Absolute is an individual, even though he is the eternal one who transcends the temporal-span of all other individuals and "preserves" all of them in their uniqueness within himself.[5]

A Royce commentator who neglects the ethico-religious aspect of Royce's thought is Murray G. Murphey in his chapter on "Josiah Royce" in *A History of Philosophy in America*;[6] a contemporary one is Bruce Kuklick. Both Murphey and Kuklick focus too much on Royce's epistemology and logic in their interpretations of his philosophy, neglecting the most significant aspects of Royce's philosophy: his philosophy of religion, his metaphysics, and his ethics.[7] Even when these commentators discuss such works as *The Problem of Christianity* and *The Sources of Religious Insight*, they tend to emphasize his logic, using it to interpret his late metaphysics of community and philosophy of religion instead of regarding it as an extension of his metaphysics and philosophy of religion.[8] Oppenheim mentions Kuklick's tendency to interpret Royce's late metaphysics of community and philosophy of religion as derivative of his logic when he writes that, along with two other shortcomings in Kuklick's perspective on Royce, "Kuklick so emphasizes the logical aspect of Royce's philosophy that he decentralizes its ethico-religious interest into simply another area of applied logic."[9] Oppenheim offers a corrective to such an interpretation of Royce's late philosophy: "[A]lthough Royce employed his logic through the *Problem [of Christianity]*—even if he kept it from the view of his ordinary audience—the *Problem* stands primarily as a work in ethics and philosophy of religion rather than a work in logic."[10]

This interpretation of Royce's philosophical development also differs from Kuklick, Murphey, and John Smith in that I do not contend that Charles S. Peirce was the principal philosopher who forced Royce to jettison his earlier absolute idealism and construct a metaphysics of community with a modified version of Peirce's theory of interpretation.[11] I will admit, though, that Peirce gave Royce the terminology to express his metaphysics more forcefully and clearly than he had prior to immersing himself in Peirce's logic. Royce admits as much in *The Problem of Christianity*.[12] Nor does this view lessen the philosophical influence that philosophers such as Joseph LeConte, William James, Arthur Schopenhauer, Plato, G. W. Leibniz, Benedict de Spinoza, G. W. F. Hegel, and Hugo Münsterberg had on Royce's intellectual development.

Yet, I contend, along with such contemporary Royce scholars as Randall E. Auxier, that the philosopher who was most influential in getting Josiah Royce to articulate his metaphysics of community in its late form is George Holmes Howison. Indeed, a few Roycean scholars, such as Auxier and Gary L. Cesarz,[13] credit Howison for being significant to the history of philosophy only for being Royce's philosophical foil at a crucial period in his intellectual development. This assessment of Howison is not meant as an insult to him or his philosophy. I personally think of him as an innovative philosophical idealist. However, the above description of his contribution to the history of philosophy is the most accurate, given the available historical evidence and the consequent history of philosophical thought. As Auxier puts it in his introduction to the first volume of *Critical Responses to Josiah Royce, 1885–1916*:

> The drift of Royce's thought from 1895 to 1916, away from an unqualified absolutism and toward a clearer commitment to personalistic community, can be read as a response to Howison's criticisms.... Perhaps it turns out that Howison's most enduring contribution to the history of philosophy was to serve as a persistent bee in Royce's philosophical bonnet. But if Howison was such

a bee, he was only the most vigorous member of an entire hive that finally chased Royce from the arid land of absolute idealism into a cool lake of finitistic, personalistic, temporal thinking.[14]

In this chapter, I intend to argue that because Howison serves as Josiah Royce's philosophical foil during his "middle" period, Royce's idealism gradually becomes more similar to Howison's personal idealism. In this respect I disagree with Auxier's assertion that Royce ceased to be an idealist in the last few years of his life and that "Royce did not move toward Howison's view—a unique form of idealistic metaphysical pluralism."[15] I would say, instead, that Royce's late metaphysics, with its accompanying realistic and process tendencies, is still idealistic, contrary to Howison's assessment of Royce's thought in 1916 and Auxier's assessment of Royce's late thought. Royce's idealism did cease to be idealistic in the nineteenth-century neo-Hegelian sense. Royce's late idealism is one that focuses on the significance of persons and the personal categories that they use to interpret reality—for example, intentionality, contingency, concern, curiosity, awe, bewilderment, and wonder—instead of focusing on the necessarily rational structure of reality assessable to the human intellect. That is, Royce comes to realize that we encounter the world as being a personal one—sometimes welcoming, other times confrontational, but ultimately a community of persons trying to approximate the ideal of the Beloved Community in their lives with one another.

By doing this in his constructive metaphysics, Royce shifted his idealism from an apparently sterile epistemology and an insightful yet cumbersome and awkward metaphysics to a more existential and phenomenological ethico-religious idealism—modifying his initial "self-representative system of selves" metaphysics and transforming this initial metaphysics to an interpretative, communal one where finite persons and the Interpreter Spirit of the Community of Interpretation are in communion with one another.

By the publication of *The Problem of Christianity* in 1913, Royce's idealism becomes remarkably similar to Howison's personal idealism in his second revised and enlarged edition of *The Limits of Evolution* (1904). In other words, Royce's late idealism, like Howison's personal idealism, emphasizes (a) the irreducible plurality of (human) persons while simultaneously (b) upholding the communal unity of persons in the ideal "City of God." According to this model of communal unity of persons as being an ideal City of God, God represents the ideal unification of all ethico-religious ideals that we are compelled to recognize, cherish, and yearn to actualize in our daily lives. This gives me a firm philosophical basis to compare Royce's personalism with both Howison's personal idealism and Boston personalism in more detail in the subsequent chapters.

George Holmes Howison, the First Personal Idealist

To understand George Holmes Howison's relentless attack[16] on Royce's "absolute" idealism and its supposed Hegelian pantheism, at the legendary "Conception of God" debate at the University of California, Berkeley, in 1895, we have to delve into Howison's philosophical shift from being a St. Louis Hegelian to the founder of American personal idealism.[17] This shift began, according to Ralph Tyler Flewelling, "as early as March 1, 1875" when Howison wrote a letter to William Torrey Harris criticizing Kant, J. G. Fichte, Hegel, and Harris himself for their overemphasis on impersonal reason and insufficient attention to individual autonomy.[18]

This 1875 criticism of the Hegelianism of his era signaled Howison's gradual drift away from St. Louis Hegelianism. This letter serves as an early indicator that he held suspect any philosophical position that did not recognize the reality of unique moral persons as distinct beings. Even in 1875 he had no tolerance for any metaphysics that reduced the irreducible plurality of persons either to momentary manifestations of the Absolute (i.e., Spinoza, Hegel) or pale facsimiles of some "Transcendent Self" (i.e., Kant and his successors).

Howison's shift from his St. Louis Hegelianism to his signature pluralistic idealism, which he labeled "personal idealism"[19] in the "Conception of God" debate, did not occur immediately after he wrote this letter. In fact, James McLachlan notes, "In 1885 Howison still claimed to be a Hegelian. But for him Hegel is the defender of the concept of the individual persons. In 1885 he was still maintaining before a Berkeley audience that Hegel was not a pantheist."[20] When Howison, "the former Hegelian-turned-pluralistic-personalist," unleashed his personal idealism publicly in 1895, he thought of himself as more than the founder of a philosophical position; he thought of himself as a philosophical prophet who had witnessed the truth.[21]

What was Howison's personal idealism? Without discussing his initial presentation of his personal idealism in *The Conception of God: A Philosophical Discussion Concerning the Nature of the Divine Idea as a Demonstrable Reality* (1895) or his most systematic articulation of his philosophy, *The Limits of Evolution*, we can get to the heart of Howison's personal idealism. Ralph Tyler Flewelling and James McLachlan have both traced the evolution of Howison's philosophical thought from St. Louis Hegelianism to personal idealism in his letters to William Torrey Harris over an almost twenty-year timespan, particularly in his letters to Harris between 1892 and 1893.[22]

First, Howison's personal idealism is a pluralistic philosophy that denounces any philosophical position that attempts to deny the undeniable reality of human persons as individual, autonomous moral beings or the personality of God. This leads Howison to abandon Hegelianism and any other type of absolute idealism, officially in a letter to W. T. Harris dated June 8, 1892, where he attacked "Royce's version of absolute idealism as 'hopeless pantheism'" because "Royce's 'infinite self' is always our dimly 'Transcendent Self,' and one might as well say that '*we* have no true self at all.'"[23] What offended Howison most about Royce's philosophical position was that "it violated his [Howison's] religious and ethical sensibilities, his deep regard for the sacred primacy of personhood."[24] In this spirit Howison wrote to W. T. Harris:

> And the most depressing sign about his thinking is that he seems perfectly aware how this makes no provision either for immortality or for real freedom, and yet he appears to have no uneasiness under it, but to contemplate this ghastly destiny of ours with a complacency even savoring of self-satisfaction."[25]

On April 25, 1895, Howison gave Harris an official declaration of his allegiance to a personal idealism that upholds the "primacy of persons": "And when I wrote that I thought Alcott's doctrine was preferable to Hegel's, and even to your own, I did not of course mean his 'lapse' theory, but his remarkable doctrine, too little developed and too little appreciated, that material creation *must be somehow through the creation of persons.*"[26] This excerpt from Howison's April 25, 1895, letter expresses the second essential element of his personal idealism: all *Wissenschaft* is derivative of our interpersonal interactions with other persons and with the Divine Person. To recap, before "The Conception of God" debate we learn that Howison became a pluralistic idealist who held that human persons were irreducibly plural and that all human scientific knowledge is constructed out of our interpersonal interactions with other persons.

The 1895 "Conception of God" Debate

The above section sets the stage for Howison's confrontation with Josiah Royce at the 1895 Berkeley Philosophical Union debate, which at the time was considered to be "the most celebrated event in the Union's history."[27] We can think of it as a precursor to what we know today as an "author meets critics" session at a professional philosophy conference. And the book that the critics commented on was Royce's ten-year-old book, *The Religious Aspect of Philosophy*.

Despite the participation of Sidney Mezes of the University of Texas and Joseph LeConte of the University of California, Berkeley, the "Conception of God" debate was essentially a debate between Howison, the pluralistic idealist, and Royce, the preeminent monistic idealist. Instead of reconstructing the entire debate between Royce and Howison in *The Conception of God*, I will depend primarily on some recent essays concerning the "Conception of God" debate to outline the general gist of the philosophical disagreement between Royce and Howison on this occasion. These essays, with the exception of two of them,[28] were published in *The Personalist Forum*'s Special Issue on the "Conception of God" debate and the relevance of Royce.[29]

James McLachlan depends on Howison's Introduction to *The Conception of God* to delineate the essential disagreement between Royce and Howison. He focuses his analysis of the Royce–Howison debate on their differing answers to the third question posed on that occasion, namely, "[w]hether [Royce's conception of God] is compatible with the autonomy of moral action which mankind . . . has come to appreciate as the vital principle of all personality"[30]:

> On the third question, Howison says that Royce and he are radically opposed. Howison maintains that in Royce's position there is a chasm that is incapable of closure between the immanence of God and the real personality and moral autonomy of created minds. Royce disagreed, denying that there is such a chasm. He claims that "a Divine self-consciousness continuously inclusive of our consciousness is demanded if a knowable God is to be proved, and that its existence is not only compatible with the existence of included conscious Selves, but directly provides for them, imparts to them as its own member its own freedom, and thus gives them all the autonomy permissible in a world that is moral." For Howison the key question in "The Conception of God" debate is: can the moral autonomy of individuals be preserved by a monistic conception of the Absolute? Royce said yes, Howison, no.[31]

McLachlan proceeds to explain Royce's argument for the conception of God. He claims, rightly, that in "The Conception of God" Royce gives the "most impressive form" of his Possibility of Error argument, originally mentioned in *The Religious Aspect of Philosophy*.[32]

In *The Religious Aspect of Philosophy,* Royce contends that error is a real phenomenon. He argues against the phenomenalist notion that error is due to the fact that some aspects of an object remain unknown to us because we only have the ability to perceive and conceive an object within certain parameters. These parameters include such things as our eyesight, our auditory sensitivity, our tactile perception, our psychological temperament, and our familiar interpretative modes of categorizing the world (which accept certain phenomena as intelligible, others as unintelligible, and still others as unconceivable or unimaginable).[33] Yet, if something remains unknowable to us, does that mean that it is unknowable forever? Could error be based on something that is forever unknowable? Royce would say that something that is forever unknowable to all minds is an absurd notion; to say that error is based on something that is, in principle, unknowable to any mind whatever is to say something unintelligible.

Gabriel Marcel captures Royce's sentiments on this issue when he writes in *Royce's Metaphysics*, "How can we err about the unknowable?"[34] Marcel rightly notes that for Royce we cannot err about the unknowable. But what is unknowable for finite beings at this particular time is not unknowable per se. Royce thinks that an ultimate mediator, an All-Knower, exists who ensures that our ideas either conform to and effectively mold reality or fail to refer to actual states of affairs and the potentialities embedded in them. Otherwise we would have no ontological foundation for our epistemic judgments about the world; that is, we would not have any way to verify the truth or falsity of our ideas about the world.

In the "Possibility of Error" chapter of *The Religious Aspect of Philosophy*, Royce demonstrates the epistemic necessity of there being a third party to mediate between our ideas about x and the objective reality of x via his John–Thomas argument. Marcel recounts that Royce's John–Thomas argument originates in a humorist's remark that a conversation between John and Thomas involves not just two persons, but six persons.[35] Table 1 shows a diagram of this argument as Marcel explicates it, with a few additional editorial comments.[36]

The explanation in Table 1 lets us appreciate the profound insight of Marcel's explication of Royce's Possibility of Error argument. Since we cannot account for the reality of error by appealing to realist conceptions of knowing an object, we have to say either that our ideas do not conform to any state of affairs in the world beyond our perceptual and cognitive capacities or that there is some infinite entity who determines the truth or falsity of our ideas. Royce opts for the latter. Marcel summarizes Royce conclusion in the Possibility of Error argument.

> "John and Thomas should be present to a third thinker whose thought should include them both" and . . . "time is once for all

TABLE 1. THE SIX "PERSONS" OF JOSIAH ROYCE'S
JOHN–THOMAS ARGUMENT.

(1) 'Real' John (i.e., the totality of "John" as an absolutely unique locus of experience consisting of every experience occurring in John's life from his birth, or even from the moment of sentience in his mother's womb, to the present—*John as absolute particular*).[a]	(4) 'Real' Thomas (i.e., the totality of "Thomas" as an absolutely unique locus of experience consisting of every experience occurring in Thomas's life from his birth, or even from the moment of sentience in his mother's womb, to the present—*Thomas as absolute particular*).[a]
(2) John's image of himself (i.e., John's interpretation of the events, or signs, that occurred to him throughout his life, especially those events that he remembers consciously and appropriates into some hopefully coherent self-identity).[b]	(5) Thomas's image of himself (i.e., Thomas's interpretation of the events, or signs, that occurred to him throughout his life, especially those events that he remembers consciously and appropriates into some hopefully coherent self-identity).[b]
(3) Thomas's image of John (i.e., Thomas's interpretation of John).	(6) John's image of Thomas (i.e., John's interpretation of Thomas).

(2) and (3) only know (1) partially because of the limits of finite beings and their cognition; the same is true of the relation between (4), (5), and (6)—i.e., (5) and (6) only know (4) partially. Only the Absolute Experience knows or experiences (1) and (2) completely as absolute particulars who participate in the Absolute Experience, or as Royce calls this in the "Supplementary Essay" to the first volume of *The World and the Individual* "actual infinity." (Royce calls this actual infinity, "the Community of Interpretation," in *The Problem of Christianity*.) Like the Community of Interpretation, the Absolute as actual infinity is the never-ending, always dynamic community of beings interrelated with one another in a holistic self-referential system.

[a] "Absolute particular" is a term inspired by D. G. Leahy's presentation at the Seventh International Conference on Persons, "The Person as Absolute Particular," August 2003. It refers to any irreducible and irreplaceable being, especially an ethical Self (i.e., person).

[b] Remember, for Royce there is no knowledge of oneself through introspection; i.e., we have no immediate knowledge of anything, including ourselves. Self-knowledge is always an interpretative act performed on us by ourselves.

present in all its moments to a universal all-inclusive thought." In this total consciousness the real John and his image of Thomas, the real Thomas and his image of John, enter as integral parts. This complete consciousness of the fragmentary intentions of two individuals is their real relationship, and confers upon the judgment one has about the other all it contains of truth and error. Error is an incomplete thought which the higher mind (which understands that thought in itself with the object it refers to) knows has failed in its intended task, and which is on the contrary fully realized in the higher mind.[37]

In "The Conception of God," Royce still accepts the conclusions of the Possibility of Error argument first mentioned in *The Religious Aspect of Philosophy*. However, as Cesarz rightly claims, Royce's argument for the existence of God in "The Conception of God" differs from his Possibility of Error argument in *The Religious Aspect of Philosophy* in that he shifts his emphasis from the possibility of error to the actuality of ignorance and of partial experience to demonstrate God's existence.[38] That is, these two arguments differ due to the fact that the Possibility of Error argument focuses primarily on the undeniable epistemic reality of error to demonstrate God's existence while the second argument focuses more on our lived, existential experience of finitude, ignorance, and incompleteness to demonstrate God's existence. Indeed, Cesarz is perhaps the first philosopher to distinguish clearly between Royce's epistemic argument from error in *The Religious Aspect of Philosophy* and his relational ontological argument from the partiality and incompleteness of our lived experience in his "Conception of God" essay.

According to Royce's relational ontological argument, then, we first consciously have an absolute experience once we become aware that we are dependent on other persons and non-personal beings to know ourselves and our world. Yet, the totality of finite persons in community does not know the *totum simul* of reality; their knowledge of themselves and the world is still partial and incomplete. This is where Royce's shift of emphasis from an abstract epistemological argument for God's existence in *The Religious Aspect of Philosophy* to an experiential and relational argument for God's existence as Absolute Experience in "The Conception of God" comes into play. In this relational ontological argument for God's existence, Royce ceases to establish the concrete reality of God in primarily epistemic terms and instead refers to our awareness that all of our encounters with others and self-knowledge is partial and incomplete as the origin for our experience of a transcendent Beyond that holds all past, present, and future events within himself.

This shift of emphasis in his argument for God's existence could be traced back to at least 1888, when he wrote marginalia in his copy of James Martineau's *A Study of Religion* while sailing to Australia and New Zealand for several months under orders from his doctor to cure his melancholy. In perhaps the most significant section of his marginalia in his copy of Martineau's text, Royce indicated his shift from demonstrating God's reality epistemologically to having God be a concrete participant in the community of "knowers"—or, as Royce calls the community of knowers in *The Problem of Christianity*, "community of interpreters."[39] While responding to Martineau's criticism of his "universal thought" and Theodore Parker's abstract Infinite, Royce felt as though he needed "to concretize and enliven his Logos [or Absolute] by getting into intersubjective relation with it, as 'Alter Ego.'"[40] Royce even built his subsequent metaphysics—from *The Spirit of Modern Philosophy* (1892) to his last works on metaphysics in 1916—around an appreciative "divine living Self."[41] By being the central component in all of Royce's subsequent metaphysical (not to mention ethical, logical, and religious) thought this "divine living Self" has tremendous ontological import.

Indeed, this concretization of Royce's Absolute into a divine living self transforms Royce's entire philosophy from being an epistemic-oriented philosophy to being an ontological and existential-oriented one that affirms his 1883 ethico-religious insight, even though he continued to write as though he was primarily concerned with epistemology and, occasionally, mathematical logic.[42] By 1895 he had already for several years described his Absolute in terms of "all-knowing and all-appreciative One . . . who affirmatively initiates, appreciates, restores, and governs community [of finite selves] through moral values even though the ignorant and alienating finite selves, by their free decisions, sometimes stray from loyal realization of moral values."[43] This shift is where Royce's philosophy and argumentation acquire its ontological posture and its dependence on experiential evidence to substantiate its contentions.

Here is Royce's relational ontological argument, as expressed in "The Conception of God": We experience a world beyond ourselves that we encounter daily. We experience natural beings that we had no part in creating, such as the Blue Ridge Mountains or the Grand Canyon. For example, I experience these beings not merely as self-constructed artifacts, but as the result of many minds and non-minded processes interacting with one another, most of which interact with one another independently of me. If I were to accept the philosophical position that the world is solely a creation of my mind alone or a community of human minds and their ideas, then what would account for the fact that we often experience things beyond our conscious willing? Royce would probably reformulate the above question this way: What guarantees that I experience anything beyond myself or beyond a hypothetical world constructed solely by my intellect or the consensus of a group of persons?

Royce probably would answer the previous questions along these lines. First, I experience the world as a categorical fact; I cannot deny that I experience something beyond myself. Even the conditions for such a denial imply that if I experience a doubt, there is something beyond myself sustaining me in my doubt. I am not even self-sufficient enough to sustain this doubt without depending on an external agent. I have to encounter other persons and non-minded (i.e., non-personal) beings to have an awareness of myself as a person because I become conscious of myself as a unique self only as a result of my contrast with other beings.[44] But are not these external persons and non-personal beings finite, also? As Royce demonstrates in his original Possibility of Error argument, no finite being could ever experience us exhaustively; that is, its knowledge of us (and our self-knowledge, I might add) is only partial.

Again we are thrown back to our original question: "What experiences us and all other finite beings in our totality?" Royce answers that undeniable sensitivity to a Beyond, of a being who preserves us, points to an Absolute Experience that experiences the totality of our universe as a concrete fact, as a genuine unity of all past and present finite experiences, couched in possibilities not yet actualized or imagined.[45] As such, God preserves a dynamic, vibrant relationship between actual experience and possible experiences, including those possible experiences that are not tied to any actual state of affairs or conceivable by any existent being but are still recognized by the Absolute as genuine (i.e., real) possible experiences or, as Royce calls these possible experiences, "ideal truth."[46] Thus, this Absolute Experience is "one self-determined and consequently absolute and organized whole."[47]

For Royce, this Absolute Experience is not only a philosophical conception, but a being whom we encounter in our concrete, lived experience. This Absolute Experience holds all reality within himself, yet upholds the irreducible uniqueness of every being. Additionally, for Royce this Absolute Experience is the God of Christian theism. It is God, as Absolute Experience, who unifies the fragmentary experiences of finite beings into a coherent whole.

In other words, Royce contends, quite persuasively, that we know that God exists through our experience of an eternal, infinite other as the ever-beyond, yet immanent presence, in our finite lives, cushioning our fallibility and finitude in the unified experiences of all finite beings in the real. While in the throes of contemplating this ever-beyond, yet immanent presence, Royce tells us of our intimately personal relationship with the Absolute:

> Where in our human world does God get revealed?—what manifests his glory? I answer: Our ignorance, our fallibility, our imperfection, our experience of longing, of strife, of pain, of error, —yes, of whatever, as finite, declares that its truth lies in its limitation, and so lies beyond itself. These things, wherein we taste the bitterness of our finitude, are what they are because they mean more than they contain, imply what is beyond them, refuse to exist by themselves, and, at the very moment of confessing their own fragmentary falsity, assure us of the reality of that fulfillment which is the life of God.[48]

The Conception of God is the first published work in which Royce explicitly mentions that God is both the preserver of the interrelated system of finite beings and a Personal Self.[49] Yet, Royce thinks that the most essential insights from the moral and religious traditions of Judaism and Christianity are conceivable in the form of a philosophical conception of God where God is regarded as an omniscient being.[50] This is why Royce would say that his philosophical theology is distinctly theistic, and not pantheistic. It is not the conception of any Unconscious Reality [unlike F. H. Bradley's Absolute], into which finite beings are absorbed; nor of a Universal Substance in whose law our ethical independence is lost; nor an Ineffable Mystery, which we can only silently adore. On the contrary, every ethical predicate that the highest religious faith of the past has attributed to God is capable of exact interpretation in terms of my present view. For my own part, then, while I wish to be no slave of any tradition, I am certainly disposed to insist that what the faith of our fathers has genuinely meant by God, is, despite all the blindness and all the unessential accidents of religious tradition, identical with the inevitable outcome of a reflective philosophy.[51]

This is the argument that George Holmes Howison confronts in his critical response to Royce's "The Conception of God" address. In his remarks to those attending the 1895 Union debate, entitled "The City of God, and the True God as Its Head," Howison lashes out at Royce, venting all the pent-up rage he has held over the last several years and attacking a philosophical position that he considered impious and dangerous. Despite having these feelings, Howison did respect Royce as a philosopher and a colleague along with agreeing that Royce's argument for God's existence is a devastating one against Spenserian and positivist agnosticism.[52]

As I mentioned above, Howison disagreed with Royce on the question whether a Roycean Absolute is compatible with persons being genuinely self-legislating (i.e., autonomous) moral selves. Without describing Howison's alternative to Royce's conception of God in detail,[53] I will describe Howison's central argument against Royce's idealism as stated in this often-quoted passage from his "The City of God and the True God as Its Head" essay in *The Conception of God*:

> But if the Infinite Self *includes* us all, and all our experiences,—sensations and sins, as well as the rest,—in the unity of one life, and includes us and them *directly*; if there is but one and the same final Self for us each and all; then, with a literalness indeed appalling, He is we, and we He; nay, He is *I*, and *I* am He. And I think it will appear later, from the nature of the argument by which the Absolute Reality as Absolute Experience is reached, that the exact

and direct way of stating the case is baldly: *I am He.* Now, if we read the conception in the first way, what becomes of our ethical independence?—what, of our *personal* reality, our righteous and reasonable responsibility—responsibility to which we *ought* to be held? Is not He the sole *agent*? Are we anything but the steadfast and changeless modes of His eternal thinking and perceiving? Or, if we read the conception in the second way, what becomes of *Him*? Then, surely, He is but another name for *me*; or for any one of *you*, if you will. And how can there be talk of a Moral Order, since there is but a single mind in the case?—we cannot legitimately call that mind a *person*.[54]

While Royce thinks that his conception of God as Absolute Experience is compatible with our being genuinely autonomous moral selves, Howison thought that Royce's arguments lead to "one of two undesirable ends: either the individual knower is omniscient; or, the individual knower is annulled and taken up into the omniscience of the absolute experience."[55] Thus for Howison, even if Royce's arguments do not lead us to solipsism, his conception of God would destroy individuality and give us a dreary metaphysical pantheism. Stephen Tyman explains Howison's concern over the consequences of Royce's Absolute as being a legitimate conception of God:

> Howison's fear was that by the time the Absolute standpoint rolls around, the only person left standing is the Absolute. But the Absolute is no person at all. The individual gets completely dissolved in the universal One, and all that is decisive, all that is distinctive in the individual's capacity to choose, is lost in the great impersonal ocean of Being. This, for Howison, was the price of pantheism.[56]

Furthermore, Howison rightly contended that Royce's argumentation does not demonstrate the necessity of such a being as his Absolute in logical terms alone. Consequently, Royce's arguments cannot depend solely on logical validity to substantiate their conclusion, but on our experiential awareness and moral experience of an interdependent, transhistorical, and superhuman community of selves.[57] And without Royce's appeal to our felt, existential awareness of such a divine whole and our dependence on him for our existence, his argumentation and its conclusions would be unconvincing.

So we cannot argue for the existence of an Absolute without first experiencing the world as an interrelated community of distinct selves, as a dynamic, relational whole, and this experience is not a purely logical one, but a moral and religious one. Thus we cannot demonstrate God's existence epistemologically, but we can say that there is experiential warrant for believing in God's existence.

Yet, how would I prove the existence of a Roycean Absolute to a solipsist, an agnostic, an atheist, or a non-Judeo-Christian religious adherent? By referring to our common experience of the world as partial, fragmentary, and incomplete, yet still dependent on something other than our fragmentary experience to be real? Could such an existential appeal ring true to someone who does not believe in the Judeo-Christian religious tradition? Howison seemed to think not. In contrast, Royce tends to think that such existential appeal rings true even for those who were not in the Judeo-Christian tradition, since he thinks that to deny the unity of all finite beings in a whole, with some transhistorical ontological function preserving this whole, is absurd and denies the reality of some of our most common moral experiences. Royce would contend later in his life that even atheists could contribute to the Absolute Experience by being committed to ideals that benefited not only themselves, but also allowed others in their community to pursue ennobling life projects, commitments, and desires.[58]

Indeed, this is why Howison's criticism of Royce's conception of God is mistaken. While Howison did think that an existential choice was essential for an adequate metaphysics, he was too wedded to Kantian formalism to appreciate the radically existential and experiential basis of Royce's entire thought. Even though Royce often used neo-Kantian terminology, sounding like Fichte, Schilling, and even Hegel at times, Royce was never a neo-Kantian in the strictest sense of the term; his principal interlocutor in German philosophy was most likely Schopenhauer.[59] Kant was a secondary in significance in Royce's idealism, and Hegel appears to be a distant third.[60] Royce had, in many ways, unwittingly advanced beyond nineteenth-century German idealism when Howison launched his attack on Royce's conception of God. Along with Auxier and Cesarz, I would say that Howison was really attacking Royce's 1885 Possibility of Error argument and not his later ontological one. What made Royce's later ontological argument so novel was that he initially did not posit the existence of an Absolute Experience. Instead, he only asserts that there is a possibility that such a being was real because we experience an ever-distant yet immanent Beyond, which transcends and unites all of our partial experiences of ourselves and the world into a coherent whole. Through this experiential awareness of such a whole uniting all partial, finite experience within himself, coupled with his uses of *reductio ad absurdum* argumentation, Royce establishes the validity of his contention that such a being is real.[61]

In doing this, he advanced the metaphysical thesis that our universe is most intelligible when we regard reality as a matrix of interrelated beings interpreted by an Absolute who preserves those relations and perpetually projects these objectified relations into the present so that our present experience is, as John Dewey says, "funded experience." That is, our present experience has meaning to us because we interpret it in light of our past—the life commitments we have chosen to pursue, the events we have judged to be life-altering, and so on. The past is real to the extent that it is preserved in the universe for us in the present to access and interpret. Ironically, Oppenheim articulates Royce's initial answer to Howison's 1895 criticism of his conception of God (and, by extension, his "Supplementary Essay" added to *The Conception of God* in 1897) in his intellectual biography of Royce's 1888 voyage to Australia and New Zealand, *Royce's Voyage Down Under*:

> The Infinite Alter Ego is viewed as a superhuman personal Subject, different from each finite self, yet being the ultimate center of identification for each self since the latter regards the Infinite Alter Ego as its own Other Self. . . . [T]his relationship to the Infinite Alter Ego runs through the whole human community as a rule, nonindividual, shared life that mediates between every member and the Infinite Alter Ego.[62]

Yet Royce did not make this case in *The Conception of God* or its "Supplementary Essay" because he had yet to express his philosophy in a language that articulated what he actually wanted to say. He would not have this philosophical vocabulary available to him until 1912, when he synthesized his ethico-religious insight with a modified Peircean theory of interpretation. However, this Peircean shift in Royce's thought, as I mentioned earlier, did not alter Royce's essential philosophical insight. He wrestled with his early period's religious insight (the existence of an All-Knower) and his middle period's metaphysical insight (that individuality is genuinely preserved and nurtured in the Absolute since the Absolute is the preserver of the past, fellow-sufferer in the present, and guarantor that the future is real) to get to his metaphysics of community, with the act of interpretation as its central feature. Royce would not have had to wrestle seriously with the consequences of his novel philosophical idealism had it not been for Howison's influential criticism of his idealism in 1895.

TWO

HAUNTED BY HOWISON'S CRITICISM: THE BIRTH OF ROYCE'S LATE PHILOSOPHY

How did this prolonged debate with Howison motivate Royce to drift away from his earlier apparent absolute idealism? W. H. Werkmeister contends that the 1895 Union debate

> had undoubtedly much to do with the progressive modification of [Royce's original] position. Royce's reply to his critics [in the "Supplementary Essay" appended to the 1897 version of *The Conception of God*], as well as his subsequent Gifford Lectures [these lectures were published as *The World and the Individual*], show clearly the new emphasis. Some years later, in *The Philosophy of Loyalty*, Royce strikes a still different note and begins a line of argumentation which leads ultimately, in *The Problem of Christianity*, to the formulation of a philosophy of life which in many respects is strikingly similar to the philosophy of Howison; for Royce's conception of the "Beloved Community" at least parallels Howison's idea of an "Eternal Republic" of spirits.[1]

One could say, then, as W. H. Werkmeister does in *A History of Philosophical Ideas in America*:

Royce is at first occupied exclusively with the cognitive side of human experience. In time, however, the emphasis shifts. Will and purpose are projected ever more strongly into the foreground, while the philosopher's interest in cognition recedes. Royce himself once said that his "deepest motives and problems" have always "centered about the Idea of the Community;" his writings, on the other hand, show that this idea has only gradually come to clear consciousness in his writings.[2]

Royce's initial response to Howison's criticism of his conception of God, and by extension his entire idealism, is in his classic essay "The Problem of Job" in *Studies of Good and Evil* (1898).[3] Indeed, I claim that in this essay Royce sets the foundation for all of his subsequent philosophy, because it is the first essay in which his ethico-religious insight ceases to be in the background and illuminates his entire philosophy, breathing new life into the "dry bones" of his absolute idealism.

Royce had thought of his philosophy as one whose concept referred to the vitality of our lived religious and ethical experiences. Unfortunately, he did not articulate this well in *The Religious Aspect of Philosophy*. Many critics, including William James and, of course, Howison, thought that he had mummified ethico-religious life in an abstract Absolute and imprisoned it in the sepulcher of Hegelian dialectics. While sailing to Australia and New Zealand for several months in 1888 under orders from his doctor to alleviate his depression, Royce wrote to William James:

> I have largely straightened out the big metaphysical tangle about continuity, freedom, and the world-formula, which, as you remember, I had aboard with me when I started, and I am ready to amuse you with a metaphysical speculation of a very simple, but, as now seems to me, of a very expansive nature, which does more to make the dry bones of my "Universal Thought" live than any prophesying that I have heretofore had the fortune to do. The fields of speculation are very wide and romantic, after all, and great is the fun of bringing down new game. I must live to tell you about this new specimen, at any rate. But I despair of describing it to you in this letter. I must wait until we meet.[4]

This means that I do not think that Royce's distinction between "appreciation" and "description" in *The Spirit of Modern Philosophy* was the insight that breathed life into the dry bones of his philosophy, as John Clendenning does;[5] it served only as a gusty wind that swayed the trees in an already blooming oasis. Even though he had already moved beyond his apparent absolute idealism of *The Religious Aspect of Philosophy* by 1888, he did not even realize that he had stumbled upon an experiential and existential idealism—a relational proto-process philosophy.

At the 1895 Union debate, his new idealism encountered its first major attack from one of the most committed and innovative idealists in America, George Holmes Howison. Immediately afterward, Royce sought to reformulate his idealism to secure the irreducible individuality of human persons while emphasizing their ontological dependence to some absolute experience.

Whether Royce realized it or not, "The Problem of Job" is the blueprint of his mature philosophy and the answer to Howison's criticisms of his philosophy. I think this is the case because I ultimately agree with John J. McDermott's assessment of Royce's response to Howison in his systematic philosophical works from "The Conception of God" to his logical essays:

> Howison says of Royce, that he is caught between pantheism and solipsism. I think Howison was right. And Howison says that so far—even given the "rich and crowded arsenal of his thinking"—so far Royce has not sustained the presence of a real, flesh and blood, erotic, neurotic individual existence, that is a *me*, a *you*, within the boundaries of his Absolute. Here also I think Howison was right; not for all the king's horses, nor all the queen's men, nor the "Supplementary Essay" to *The Conception of God*, nor *The World and the Individual*, nor the never-ending supplementary essays to those massive volumes, nor System Sigma, could overcome Howison's critique and it echoes in Davidson, and Hodgson and Peirce and James. For a possible way out look to Royce from his book on loyalty forward, and look backward to the social, historical, religious and environmental essays. There, throughout, has to be sought material for a reply to Howison.[6]

Taking McDermott's suggestion seriously, I contend that Royce did answer Howison's principal objection to his metaphysics, just not sufficiently in his systematic philosophical works, at least up to *The Problem of Christianity*. We have to read and analyze Royce's social, ethical, and religious essays for his answer to Howison's criticisms—for example, "The Problem of Job"; the last lecture of the second volume of *World and the Individual*, *The Philosophy of Loyalty*, and his *1915–16 Extension Course on Ethics*. Consequently, I will dedicate this chapter to examining Royce's philosophy up to *The Problem of Christianity* and the next chapter to examining Royce's mature philosophy, as expressed in *The Problem of Christianity* and his *1915–16 Extension Course on Ethics*.

"The Problem of Job"

Royce commentators usually analyze "The Problem of Job" primarily, if not exclusively, as Royce's initial substantive attempt to solve the philosophical problem of evil. I agree with this interpretation of the major theme of this essay. Like Leibniz's *Discourse on Metaphysics* (1686) and *Monadology* (1714), the problem of evil is the philosophical issue that guides Royce's construction of his metaphysics. Indeed, I think Royce's metaphysics would not be communal and religious if not for his intimate experience of evil and suffering, both firsthand and by those around him.[7] Since Royce's solution to the problem of evil is perhaps the best-known aspect of his philosophy, I will not give any significant attention to it. Instead, I want to extract the metaphysical kernel out of this essay.

With that I will start with an analysis of the first spiritual truth Royce mentions in "The Problem of Job":

> God is not in ultimate essence another being than yourself. He is the Absolute Being. You truly are one with God, part of his life. He is the very soul of your soul. And so, here is the first truth: When you suffer, *your sufferings are God's sufferings*, not his external work, not his external penalty, not the fruit of his neglect, but

identically his own personal woe. In you God himself suffers, precisely as you do, and has all your concern in overcoming this grief.[8]

Here is Royce's initial articulation of panentheism.[9] God is not wholly Other. God is not Absolute in the traditional sense of being radically independent. God is, first and foremost, a relational—and therefore personal—God. God is thus immanent in the world as a spirit who experiences what we experience. God is not logically identical to us finite beings; that is, we cannot say "I am he" or "He is I," contra Howison's misinterpretation of Royce's conception of God.[10] Instead, God is fellow sufferer and co-experiencer of the world. Moreover, God yearns for us to overcome our grief, for when we suffer, God suffers, too. Royce tries to clarify his panentheistic conception of God when he writes: "We ourselves exist as fragments of the absolute life, or better, as partial functions in the unity of the absolute and conscious process of the world. On the other hand, our existence and our individuality are not illusory, but are what they are in an organic unity with the whole life of the Absolute Being."[11] In short, we are only partial manifestations of life itself, expressing only a fraction of its inexhaustible, ever-dynamic, and never-ending richness in our all-too-brief lives. Yet, we remain distinct and irreducibly unique individuals within this overall life because no other being, not even God, could replace any one of us without altering the very fabric of reality and God's own self-identity. God could not be who God is without us performing our unique roles in the grand cosmic drama. Resolving this tension between individuality and divine unity within a metaphysics of community becomes the cornerstone for Royce's later philosophy.

Royce even gives us a synopsis of his subsequent philosophy in the following awe-inspiring and lengthy excerpt from "The Problem of Job." In response to someone's belief that God's triumph over evil is not his or her triumph because he or she does not experience God's triumph as mine, Royce says:

> It is your fault that you are thus sundered from God's triumph. His experience in its wholeness cannot now be yours, for you just

as you—this individual—are now but a fragment, and see his truth as through a glass darkly. But if you see his truth at all, through even the dimmest light of a glimmering reason, remember, that truth is in fact your own truth, your own fulfillment, the whole from which your life cannot be divorced, the reality that you mean even when you most doubt, the desire of your heart even when you are most blind, the perfection that you unconsciously strove for even when you were an infant, the complete Self apart from whom you mean nothing, the very life that gives your life the only value which it can have. In thought, if not in the fulfillment of thought, in aim if not in attainment of aim, in aspiration if not in the presence of the revealed fact, you can view God's triumph and peace as your triumph and peace. Your defeat will be no less real than it is, nor will you falsely call your evil a mere illusion. But you will see not only the grief but the truth, your rescue, your triumph.[12]

As we shall see in this chapter and the next, Royce's later philosophic works are an expansion of these thoughts: (1) God is immanent in the world, experiencing the world with us as we experience it; (2) God is transcendent, unifying all beings within himself; (3) we are partial, yet irreducibly individual and essential, manifestations of the divine life—that is, we are simultaneously individual beings and dependent on the Absolute for our existence; and (4) God is a triumphant, moral God who serves as the ultimate ontological ground for all of our moral efforts and ideals.

The World and the Individual

We are now in a position to approach Royce's philosophy up to *The World and the Individual*. I contend that Gabriel Marcel's explanation of Royce's Absolute, as Royce understood the Absolute at the time he wrote *Studies of Good and Evil*, is one of the most profound and accurate assessments of Royce's philosophical thought as of 1899:

> Now it can be understood how Royce can say: My world of objects, if it exists, is what my total self would acknowledge as the totality of my thoughts raised to full consciousness of their meaning. But we already know that this total self cannot be merely a

system of possible experiences because what is only possible is strictly nothing. This absolute meaning is thus actualized in the One who knows all truth in its unity, in that true and complete Person to whom anyone who conceives a world of objects is organically united. "The world is in and for a thought, all-embracing, all-knowing, universal, for which are all relations [including possibilities] and all truth, a thought that estimates perfectly our imperfect and halting thought." Absolute idealism, as conceived by Royce, leads directly to an All-Knower.[13]

Let me interrupt my explication to clarify Royce's ontological vocabulary so my description and explanation of his metaphysics remains relatively consistent. Throughout his career, Royce occasionally used the ontological terms "actual" and "actuality," which harbor the Aristotelian assumption that whatever is actual refers to whatever has existed in the past or exists currently, that is, to both actualities and potentialities in the Aristotelian sense. He also includes the term "actual" sometimes to refer to possibilities *qua* possibilities, which, as an ontological class, includes non-actualizable possibilities. For the sake of consistency, I will use the ontological vocabulary Royce uses in *Metaphysics*,[14] which is itself a clarification and revision of the ontological vocabulary he uses in the first volume of *The World and the Individual* (47–54), whenever possible. In his *Metaphysics* Royce defines "existence," and "reality" in this manner:

> Being belongs to whatever object you can define at all or think of or call to your attention. The objects of a dream have being; fictitious objects have being; round squares have being. Being as being belongs to all possible objects of inquiry or even of denial. An *entity* is that which has being.
> *Existence* has special reference to time and space. To say "X exists" means X has a place in the time-space world . . . .
> *Reality* is the name for that which has not merely being, quiddity, or a predicable character, and which has not merely existence; reality is a predicate which applies to the world as a whole, the connected and organized whole of the world. Its significance is

distinctly teleological. Reality is possessed by an object which possesses a meaning, a significance, a wholeness, a totality which need not be possessed by an object which merely exists.[15]

Unlike Royce, though, I will use the term "real" as synonymous with "being" because of the metaphysical baggage accompanying that term. Besides Royce, like most of the writings of his contemporaries in Anglo-American philosophy, restricted the word *being* was to mean "actually existent" entities. Using the term "real" will avoid the confusion involved in remembering how Royce understands "being" in a given context. Whenever appropriate, I will use the term *reality* the way Royce does in *The World and the Individual* and *Metaphysics;* other times, I might use it to mean "real" for aesthetic and rhetorical purposes.

A third issue that should be clarified before I continue my explication of Royce's philosophy is Royce's usage of the phrases "whole self" and "total self." Many readers may not be familiar with Royce's usage of these terms, since we, especially in the English-speaking world, are accustomed to restricting our philosophical discussions on the "self" to the actual self and, maybe, its immediate potentialities. When Royce says "total self" or "whole self" in his writings, however, he does not refer only to someone as an actual self, but also as an ideal self with potentialities beyond the immediate future and the hardly imaginable possibilities in the future. To demonstrate that Royce thought of the "whole self" in similar terms, here is Loewenberg's explanation of what Royce means by the expression:

> That the individual self is not a "present datum" [i.e., actual] but an "ideal," the product of an active "construction" or, in his later terminology, "interpretation," is one of Royce's cardinal teachings. It is emphasized over and over again. . . . The self of the moment without temporal extension has for Royce little meaning. "The present self," he remarks, "the fleeting individual of today, is a mere gesticulation of a self. The genuine person lives in the far-off past and future as well as in the present." "Considered simply in this passing moment of my life," so he declares, "I am hardly a self at all." . . . What, then, is the self? It is for Royce a

life "whose unity and connectedness depend upon . . . interpretation of plans, of memories, of hopes, and of deeds." It is a being which never exists as a *finished* product; it is a process which extends forward as well as backward.[16]

With these issues being sufficiently clarified for us to have a consistent rendering of Royce's ontological vocabulary, I return now to explicating Royce's philosophy.

Royce's Absolute is the pinnacle of an ethico-religious dialectic, with the Absolute emerging out of, embracing, and sustaining concrete, lived human experience and its relation to an eternal yet immanent Other. Nevertheless, many Royce scholars over the last century or so conceive of Royce's Absolute as a completed actuality in the traditional Aristotelian sense. Marcel's early study of Royce's metaphysics is perhaps the first major work on Royce's philosophy that interprets him this way. Another way to understand Royce's Absolute, however, is not as a fixed, completed actuality, but as an absolute actual experience that experiences the temporality of existence. This would lead us to interpret his absolute actual experience as including within itself the ideality of possible experiences *qua* possible experiences within the Absolute. That is, possibilities are real as possibilities for the Absolute even though we as finite beings can entertain them in our lives only as potentialities. Moreover, these possibilities are real without depending ontologically upon any actual state of affairs in the world; they are real because they reside in the Absolute. Whenever one reads "actual experience," as opposed to "possible experience," in Royce's *The World and the Individual*, remember that for him possible experience is not dependent on actual finite experiences, but on the existence of the Absolute as the one who recognizes possible experiences as possible. He reminds us in his *Metaphysics*:

> There are countless things which God might have created and which he didn't create. In dealing with the world of his ideas, the divine Will selected those of them to which the creative Idea gave the particular realization which constitutes the existence of the created world. The general relation is that of part to whole, or in terms as near to ordinary usage as you can get, the real or existent

is only a part of the possible, so far as its essence is concerned. Only a part of the essences are existent [or actually localizable in a particular being, embodied in the space-time continuum]. There are countless more that might have been, but here are only you and I. We human beings form a part of beings that might have been evolved [in God's perpetual act of interpreting the actual universe].[17]

This later description of his metaphysical schema in *World and the Individual* further demonstrates his belief that while we cannot entertain possibilities without them becoming potentialities,[18] God can, and does, retain possibilities *qua* possibilities within himself. What is possible and potential, then, are larger ontological categories than what is actual or existent in a spatio-temporal sense. Figure 1 is a diagram of the relation between possibility, potentiality, and actuality in Royce's middle and later metaphysics.

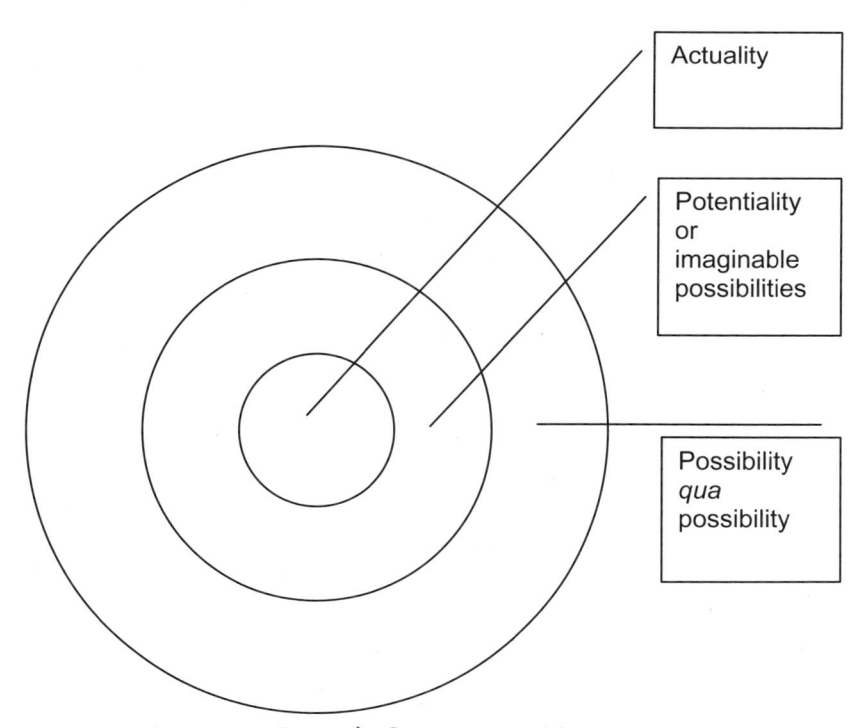

FIGURE 1. ROYCE'S CONCENTRIC METAPHYSICS

With this delineation of Royce's metaphysics we are prepared to analyze the first substantial response Royce made to Howison's criticism of his earlier "absolute" idealism (excluding his 1897 "Supplementary Essay" in the second edition of *The Conception of God*) in *The World and the Individual*. Yet, this response is not primarily in the first volume of that work, which serves as a launch pad for Royce's constructive metaphysics; it is expressed in the last lecture of the second volume. To see Royce's response to Howison we have to leap over his *reductio ad abusurdum* arguments against the three historical conceptions of Being—realism, mysticism, and critical rationalism—and focus on his description of concrete idealism. Then we have to examine his metaphysics of community in its intermediate stage of development, as articulated in the second volume of *The World and the Individual*.

According to Royce our concrete experiences—our lived experiences as beings-in-the-world—are contained in an all-inclusive absolute life that contains all past occurrences and potentialities within Him. Otherwise we would have no basis for claiming that our immediate awareness of the world has any funded meaning or has any relation to some future; all of our experiences would simply be one brute fact after another with no relation to one another—a Humean universe of atomic facts. Yet Royce is in the tradition of British empiricism, with which he agrees that experience is the origin for all human knowledge.[19]

While Royce shares a reverence for "experience" with the British empiricist tradition, he thought that they were too wed to metaphysical realism to elucidate our experience faithfully. He even felt that Berkeley, whose metaphysics most resembles his own idealism, did not go beyond the superficial empiricist analysis of our perceptions and the derivative conceptions constructed out of our sense impressions. Like other British empiricists, Berkeley did not deal with the "temporal density" of beings or the duration of an existent being's structural integrity over time. Instead, he sought to guarantee their continued existence in the mind of God without discussing the relation between temporality and God. Is God temporality itself? How does God preserve the temporal density of beings? How is God ontologically distinct from finite beings if God preserves them? These are the questions Berkeley unwittingly introduced into British and American philosophy and which Royce answers in *The World and the Individual*.

Unlike Berkeley, Royce transcends Lockean empiricism and recognizes the concrete temporal reality of God as the ontological glue that holds reality together. He also recognizes that God functions like a weaver in that God weaves the irreducible particulars who act in time and the temporal threads that are their acts into a single tapestry. Royce treats this phenomenon when he discusses the time-process as the temporal duration of every being. Indeed, every existent being is an ongoing temporal process or a series of sequential events united within a locus of experience.[20] Having an ontological locus of experience enables a being to have and maintain its structural integrity, its identity as a unique being.

The difference between minded and non-minded beings is that the former have the capacity to interpret their temporal duration, giving their lives a variety of meanings. A non-minded being does not interpret its temporal duration (i.e., length of existence); it only preserves its structural integrity until it ceases to be a unified temporal process. For example, a rock will preserve its structural integrity until some external event destroys it; however, there is no reason to think that a rock interprets its existence as being meaningful or hopeless. A rock simply is. Thus, we do not say that a rock has any meaning in-itself, or at least we cannot know the significance of a rock beyond our acts of interpretation (to use Royce's later terminology). The rock gets its meaning through acts of interpretation by minded beings, and, ultimately, by its relation to all other finite beings within the Absolute whose temporal duration is endless. In other words, the Absolute's history is temporality itself and the history of our universe. Nevertheless, each finite being has its own distinct history, which is dependent on the Absolute but not reducible to a mode of the Absolute.

How does Royce maintain the ontological distinction between finite beings and the Absolute when finite beings could not even have a history without the Absolute? He would say that a finite being is what it is because of the purpose(s) it pursues during its time span; a purpose, for Royce, is a tendency to develop in a certain direction. For ethical selves (i.e., minded beings), especially human persons, our purpose is the "life-plan" that unifies all of our prior experiences, life commitments, hopes, dreams, and yearnings into a coherent, intelligible whole.[21] Furthermore, this life-plan has to be one that an ethical self willingly chooses and actively pursues. Indeed, Royce defines ethical selfhood in this excerpt from *The World and the Individual*:

> At this instant I am indeed one with God, in the sense that in him my own absolute Selfhood is expressed. But God's will is expressed in a manifold life. And this life is a system of contrasted lives that are various even by virtue of their significant union. For true unity of meaning is best manifested in variety, just as the most intimate and wealthy friendship is that of strongly contrasting friends. And in the manifold lives that the world in its unity embodies, there is one, and only one, whose task is here hinted to me as my task, my life-plan,—an ideal whose expression needs indeed the cooperation of countless other Selves, of a social order, of Nature, and of the whole universe, but whose individual significance remains contrasted with all other individual significance. If this is my task, if this is what my past life has meant, if this is what my future is to fulfill, if it is in this way that I do God's work, if my true relation to the Absolute is only to be won through the realization of this life-plan, and through the accomplishment of this unique task, then indeed I am a Self, and a Self who is nobody else, just precisely in so far as my life has this purpose and no other. *By this meaning of my life-plan, by this possession of an ideal, by this Intent always to remain another than my fellows despite my divinely planned unity with them,—by this, and not by the possession of any Soul-Substance, I am defined and created a Self.*[22]

For Royce, then, we are neither empirical egos nor Aristotelian *ousia*, definable only in terms of our empirically observable characteristics. We are primarily the life-plans we live out in our daily lives. By choosing a life-plan which most effectively motivates us to develop our fullest potential, we fulfill a task only we as unique finite persons could fulfill: to advance the spiritual union of all persons by our recognizing the irreplaceability of all persons and by our being mindful of our dependence on one another and on the Absolute for our very existence. By doing these two things to advance the spiritual union of all persons, we should be motivated to live in ways that foster the actualization of more inclusive moral communities, which, in turn, should improve the health of our entire ecosystem—human persons, non-human persons, and non-personal (yet purposeful) cosmic processes alike.[23]

Furthermore, the Absolute, or God, is not omnipotent in the classical sense for Royce; rather, God depends on our acting out our life-plans for his will to be done at all. God has no causal power, and has only the divine allure of agapic love as the eternal Ideal to motivate us to actualize his will.[24] God as agapic love, God as ideal, is the ideal of a universe where more and more persons get the opportunity to cultivate their unique talents and pursue their diverse life-plans, or purposes, while beneficially serving the larger community of persons.[25] In his final lecture of the second volume of *World and the Individual*, Royce summarizes his entire metaphysics:

> Despite God's absolute unity, we, as individuals, preserve and attain our unique lives and meanings, and are not lost in the very life that sustains us, and that needs us as its own expression. This life is real through us all; and we are real through our union with this life. Close is our touch with the eternal. Boundless is the meaning of our nature. Its mysteries baffle our present science, and escape our present experience; but they need not blind our eyes to the central unity of Being, nor make us feel lost in a realm where all the wanderings of time mean the process whereby is discovered in the homeland of Eternity.[26]

We should remind ourselves that Royce does not restrict "purposiveness" to human persons and the divine Person alone. In the "Supplementary Essay" and second volume of Royce's *The World and the Individual*, Royce contends that all selves—ethical selves and nonethical selves alike—have purposes—either directly because they are cognitively aware of their purposes or indirectly because their purposes are not known by them but by minded beings and/or the Absolute. Accordingly, Nature, as the matrix of interrelated non-minded beings, has genuine purposes just like minded beings do.[27] Contrary to Kant, then, Nature does not have only as-if intentionality but actual intentionality. Yet Nature has no *telos* in the Aristotelian or Hegelian sense of a determinant, fixed end that it seeks to actualize completely. Nature, instead, is purposiveness because it is a component of the Real, more specifically the purposefulness of non-minded beings, which with the purposefulness of minded beings constitutes reality's immanent order.

This immanent order is one in which the objectified relations among existent beings, understood temporally as the immediate past, determine the structure of present occurrences and the potentialities invisibly couched in the present. These potentialities constitute the immediate future. Taken together, this progression of immediate past, present moment, and immediate future is an orderly, temporal process in which the immediate past becomes present and the present becomes future in a fluid temporal motion.

Nevertheless, as this temporal process extends beyond the confines of the immediate past, present moment, and immediate future, the further in the future we attempt to contemplate, the more indeterminate reality becomes.[28] Due to this inherent indeterminacy, reality becomes more and more open to radical change the further into the future we contemplate, allowing us to entertain once-unimaginable possibilities as live options for us, as ends-in-view to pursue in our lives, and to project them into the indeterminate future. This temporal process is, as I shall discuss later in this chapter, the never-ending movement of agapic love in the universe. To understand the nature of agapic love, though, we have to understand Royce's "loyalty to loyalty" as his central ethico-religious concept expressed as a moral philosophy. Let us now see how agapic love as "loyalty to loyalty" manifests itself in our lives by discussing Royce's *The Philosophy of Loyalty*.

The Philosophy of Loyalty

Instead of subjecting the reader to a detailed exegesis of *The Philosophy of Loyalty* to explicate Roycean "loyalty to loyalty," I will describe how this notion fits his into his overall philosophy, especially his metaphysics of community. "Loyalty to loyalty," or being loyal to genuine loyalty, involves respecting the diversity of moral ideals and trying to create a more hospitable environment where persons could pursue their ideals in a non-confrontational (or less confrontational) atmosphere. Living a life in pursuit of genuine loyalty lets one respect and willingly assist others as fellow persons who yearn to pursue their own loyalties, even if they are different from one's own (at least as long as these loyalties are not intentionally detrimental to other persons' loyalties—e.g., killing someone who does not believe in the same religion, or the same interpretation of religious scriptures, as you do—unless these other persons' loyalties are actively detrimental to loyalty to loyalty).[29] There are times, though, when *agape* manifests itself in the form of "tough love." The paradigmatic example of *agape* being a form of tough love is when a society has to imprison someone whose actions harm the social fabric, for example, when someone brutally assaults another person. In such cases, Royce thinks that acting in the spirit of *agape* requires us to imprison the one who brutally assaults someone else.

We should note here that not all true loyalties are conducive to creating a more inclusive moral community. An example of a loyalty that is not conducive to creating a more inclusive moral community is what Royce would call "provincial loyalty." Griffin Trotter says of natural loyalty that it is "loyalty to the ideals of some naturally occurring community with limited membership. Natural loyalty is exclusive, cultivating and/or preserving a social division between its chosen followers and other natural communities."[30] Our membership in a tribe, a region, a nation, an ethnic group, an exclusive country club, or a professional organization are examples of natural loyalty because these communities provide us with numerous ideals we could appropriate in our lives and from which we can construct our ethical Selfhood. However, these loyalties do not advance the establishment of a more inclusive moral community. That is only done by genuine loyalty, which is "loyalty to all humanity, where humanity is viewed as a (potential) community.... Loyalty to loyalty ... consciously subordinates devotion to natural communities—that is, natural loyalties—to a higher devotion to humanity. When we make this move, our natural loyalties become genuine."[31]

For Royce, then, to live consistent with a love of humanity often means to live inconsistent with familial, tribal, or societal loyalties. This commitment to remain "loyal to loyalty" echoes Emerson's famous saying:

> A foolish consistency is the hobgoblin of little minds, adored by little statesmen and philosophers and divines. With consistency a great soul has simply nothing to do. He may as well concern himself with his shadow on the wall. Speak what you think now in hard words and tomorrow speak what tomorrow thinks in hard words again, though it contradict every thing you said today.[32]

Edgar S. Brightman, an early twentieth-century Boston personalist, clarifies these sentiments first expressed by Emerson, and later by Royce, in his 1933 work *Moral Laws*:

> [D]id [Emerson] mean that all consistency is foolish? Is it not much truer to the spirit of Emerson to say that he meant the petty consistency which refuses to learn anything new or to change any opinion once adopted than that he meant the consistency of a sincere good will [i.e., a person who wills to live up to her highest and most-inclusive moral ideals]?[33]

As we have seen, Royce does not have a rule-oriented ethical theory in the sense of either utilitarianism or Kantian ethics. He learned from his own life experiences that all moral philosophy (and philosophy in general) could do is offer helpful hints here and there, such as reminding us that when we encounter a moral dilemma we should only choose the alternative that we could imagine ourselves living out and could justify to others as being the most moral one available to us at the time. In cases where an ethical dilemma forces us to choose between loyalties, Royce does not give us a hedonistic calculus or a categorical imperative; instead, he says:

> As a fact, the conscience is the ideal of the self, coming to consciousness as a present command. It says, *Be loyal.* If one asks, *Loyal to what?* The conscience, awakened by our whole personal response to the need of mankind replies, *Be loyal to loyalty.* If, hereupon, various loyalties seem to conflict, the conscience says: *Decide.* If one asks, *How decide?* conscience further urges, *Decide as I, your conscience, the ideal expression of your whole personal nature, conscious and unconscious, find best.* If one persists, *But you and I may be wrong,* the last word of conscience is, *We are fallible, but we can be decisive and faithful; and this is loyalty.*[34]

Royce's ethics is an example of a philosophical analysis of our moral experience, which focuses not only in instances of existential doubt about what to do, but also in the daily lives of ordinary persons. He states this fact of our moral experience when he writes:

> [W]hen we declared loyalty to be a supreme good for the loyal man himself, we were not speaking of a good that can come to a few men only—to heroes or to saints of an especially exalted mental type. As we expressly said, the mightiest and the humblest members of any social order can be morally equal in the exemplification of loyalty. . . . You all of you . . . know plain and wholly obscure men and women, of whom the world has never heard, and is not worthy but who have possessed and who have proved in the presence of you who have chanced to observe them, a loyalty to their chosen cause which was not indeed expressed in martial deeds, but which was quite as genuine a loyalty as that of a Samurai, or as that of Arnold von Winkelried when he rushed upon the Austrian spears. As for the ordinary expressions of loyalty, not at critical moments and in the heroic instants that come to the plainest lives, but in daily business, we are all aware how the letter carrier and the housemaid may live, and often do live, when they choose, as complete a daily life of steadfast loyalty as could any knight or king. Some of us certainly know precisely such truly great personal embodiments of loyalty in those who are, in the world's ill-judging eyes, the little ones of the community.[35]

Furthermore, according to Royce, our yearning for a spiritual union with other persons, while retaining our individuality, is not merely an unverifiable postulate. This unifying moral ideal is real and manifests itself in our daily interactions with persons who promote loyalty to loyalty by living their lives dedicated to their chosen causes. The experiential evidence that loyalty to loyalty is a real human phenomenon is almost ubiquitous in our encounters with others; we see evidence of loyalty to loyalty when we notice the trustworthy accountant who does his job well and deals fairly with her clients, the loyal friend who stays by your side when others abandon you, or the guy who helps an elderly couple stranded on the shoulder of the road because their car has a flat tire. Royce summarizes this point when he writes:

> Loyalty, then, is contagious. It infects not only the fellow-servant of your own special cause, but also all who know of this act. Loyalty is a good that spreads. Live it and you thereby cultivate it in other men. Be faithful, then, so one may say, to the loyal man: be faithful over your few things, for the spirit of loyalty, secretly passing from you to many to whom you are a stranger, may even thereby make you unconsciously ruler over many things. Loyalty to loyalty is then no unpractical cause. And you serve it not by becoming a mere citizen of the world, but by serving your personal cause. We set before you, then, no unpractical rule when we repeat our moral formula in this form: Find your own cause, your interesting, fascinating, personally engrossing cause; serve it with all your might and soul and strength; but so choose your cause, and so serve it, that thereby you show forth your loyalty to loyalty, so that because of your choice and service of your cause, there is a maximum of increase of loyalty amongst your fellow-men.[36]

I have a personal anecdote that demonstrates Royce's point about how loyalty to loyalty manifests itself in our everyday lives. From an early age, when I lived in the Tidewater region of Virginia, my mother told me stories about a local woman who dedicated her life to the Christian virtue of charity. Her name was Miss Jenny Clarkson, but everyone simply called her Miss Jenny. Miss Jenny taught my mother the meaning of genuine loyalty through her daily conduct. For example, Miss Jenny treated African Americans with dignity and respect at a time when doing so was socially unacceptable. And she helped anyone in the community who needed help. She would visit the sick. She would assist people by helping them get welfare until they could get back on their feet. She even let my parents and my oldest siblings stay on an acre of her property for a while, and when my father offered to buy that acre of land, she gave it to them. Let me repeat, she gave it to them. She asked for nothing in return. Even though the house lacked some of the basic sanitation mandatory for houses today, such as indoor plumbing, that house served its purpose well until my father could afford to move into a house with all the modern amenities which someone would have expected a house to have in August 1979, nearly a year after I was born.

My mother, in turn, acted out of loyalty to loyalty when she encountered other persons because of Miss Jenny's example. And, however infrequently I am loyal to genuine loyalty, I act out of my appreciation of my mother's dedication to genuine loyalty. My point is that without Miss Jenny and others like her teaching my mother how to be loyal to loyalty in actual practice, I would not have learned what genuine loyalty was. Miss Jenny's loyalty to loyalty was contiguous, indeed.

Royce's mature ethics, as presented in *The Philosophy of Loyalty*, expressed in detail how the ethical vision at the end of the second volume of *The World and the Individual* could manifest itself in our daily lives. Because of this, Royce's metaphysics of community emerges in its almost fully mature form in the last two lectures of *The Philosophy of Loyalty*. In the process of arguing against William James's characterization of his metaphysics as being a gross abstraction, or a fatalistic universe where all of our moral efforts are for naught, Royce defines the relationship between finite persons and the Absolute, between the finite and the Eternal.

For Royce, the Eternal is not a static, fixed entity. As we have seen in our analysis of "The Problem of Job" and *The World and the Individual*, the Eternal is the perpetual preserver of what has already occurred in the universe and what is occurring now (what I called earlier "immanent order") and the ontological space in which some possibilities first become imaginable for us and later available as viable ways of acting for us. As we act more morally toward our fellow person, the universe becomes a little more moral as well, but since the universe is always changing, our accomplishments are always temporary. Thus, we have to struggle continuously to retain the civility and moral development we currently have and, if possible, struggle to improve our moral standing. We have to inch ever-closer to embodying, even if only for a moment, the spirit of loyalty, which believes in the existence of an ever-open universe in which the unimaginable is yet possible and human betterment is always a live option.[37] As Royce expresses on this subject:

> [T]he loyal man, I think, whether he imagines himself to be a recent pragmatist or not, has a rational right to say this: My cause partakes of the nature of the only truth and reality that there is. My life is an effort to manifest such eternal truth, as well as I can, in a series of temporal deeds. I may serve my cause ill. I may conceive it erroneously. I may lose it in the thicket of this world of transient experience. My every human deed may involve a blunder. My mortal life may seem one long series of failures. But I know that my cause liveth. My true life is hid with the cause and belongs to the eternal.[38]

This sounds similar to William James's moral nightingale singing its eternal song in all sorts of different persons' hearts, spanning different time periods. This pursuit of such a moral nightingale is a lost cause, since we are destined to die and leave our accomplishments to the mercies of a precarious world and the fragility of human existence before we could ever actualize it fully, but its song still compels us to answer with concrete deeds. Sometimes these deeds even improve people's lives and advance the ideal of a universal community of the loyal.

In subsequent works, mainly in *The Sources of Religious Insight*, Royce further clarifies his conception of eternity and the eternal. This is not a remarkable shift of emphasis for Royce, for he dealt with these concepts whenever he discussed the Absolute, either as Absolute Thought or Absolute Experience. By 1911, the only thing he did was cease calling the eternal "the Absolute." He made only a minor alteration of word choice, but this virtual removal of "the Absolute" from his ontological vocabulary[39] lets the existential and phenomenological aspects of his philosophy emerge in and enliven his texts. This does not mean that he denounced his earlier idealism;[40] he only modified it to be more faithful to our experiences in the world.

Royce, on the cusp of his later philosophy, defines "eternity" as the time-inclusive and fluid totality of all temporal time-spans within the eternal. Furthermore, he identifies the divine life with a chronosynoptic vision of eternity, that is,

> *the endless whole of future time, as well as of past time, before them in one, not timeless, but time-inclusive survey, which embraces the whole of real life.* And just such a survey, and just such a life, not timeless, but time-inclusive, constitutes the eternal, which is real, not apart from time, and from our lives, but in, and through and above all our individual lives. The divine will wills in us and in all this world, with its endless past and its endless future, at once. The divine insight is not lifeless. It includes and surveys all life. All is temporal in its ceaseless flow and in its sequence of individual deeds. All is eternal in the unity of its meaning.[41]

This does not mean that the divine experiences all temporal events all at once, however; the divine does not experience the totality of the Real *"at any one moment in time."*[42] This would make our universe a block universe, and Royce always avoided portraying the universe as anything other than dynamic and open-ended.

Royce's conception of eternity, as expressed in *The Sources of Religious Insight,* is the conception of God that he tried to communicate in "The Conception of God," "The Problem of Job," *The World and the Individual, The Philosophy of Loyalty,* and in several essays from his *William James and Other Essays Concerning the Philosophy of Life.* This is what Royce tried to tell George Holmes Howison in his over-two-hundred-page "Supplementary Essay" in *The Conception of God.* God is neither a logical principle nor a noumenal existence; God is that person who enables ideals to be actualizable by finite-minded beings and who can persuade embodied-minded beings to act morally in the world. Again, Royce hammers the point that advocating such a conception of God as the interpreter spirit of the Beloved Community and preserver of the universe "is not to deny our freedom and our initiative."[43] In fact, he contends: "The divine will wills me, precisely in so far as it wills that, in each of my individual deeds, I should then and there express my own unique, and in so far free, choice."[44]

Thus, when we experience the eternal as a real presence in our lives, we recognize that we can choose to act on the impossible Ideal, the universal siblinghood of the Loyal, in our daily lives and, in doing so, create more humane communities. This moment of recognition is the moment when we hear the eternal nightingale sing in our ears, when the impossible Ideal becomes possible, beckoning us to live as though it were already here.[45] In "eternity" we dance with the Everlasting Eternal and participate in the Beloved Community insofar as we act in the spirit of genuine loyalty.[46] With Royce's act of redefining "eternity" as simultaneously, (1) the dynamic, all-inclusiveness that preserves the past, experiences the present, and anticipates the future within itself and (2) an existential phenomenon wherein finite ethical individuals experience the divine whole and become participants in the universal community of the loyal, Royce's thought sheds the last remnants of nineteenth-century idealism and ushers in his late philosophy.

THREE

ROYCE'S LATE PHILOSOPHY

We are now in a position to see how Royce's later philosophy addresses Howison's 1895 criticism of his idealistic metaphysics. Since I will analyze just those elements of Royce's later writings that seem to address Howison's criticism directly, I will leave aside, for example, such significant Roycean concepts as atonement, redemption, and reconciliation in his *The Problem of Christianity*.[1] Instead I turn to the significance of the will to interpret for the constitution of human personhood and that of the divine Self, as well as how Royce's late conception of human personhood addresses Howison's critique of his idealistic metaphysics. The chapter ends with a comparison of Howison's personal idealism and Royce's idealistic metaphysics, showing that by 1915 Royce's metaphysics of community became very similar to Howison's personal idealism.

Reading Royce's The Problem of Christianity *as a Reply to Howison*

To see how Royce's *The Problem of Christianity* could be interpreted as part of his two-decade-long reply to Howison's criticism, we should examine Royce's conception of the will to interpret and how it functions in human life and constitutes the divine life.

The will to interpret enables us to build communities with others where there were once none; it also serves as our means for establishing communities of memory, where persons agree to interpret certain past events in a similar way, and communities of hope, where persons share similar anticipations for the future.[2] No community, for Royce, is a genuine one without being both a community of memory and one of hope. This makes sense because without sharing both memory and anticipation of the future, we have only an aggregate of persons in the same geographical location. This non-community is what Royce calls a society.[3] However, the will to interpret is more than the force motivating us to establish communities of persons. When recognized as the spirit of the Beloved Community immanent in the world, it is what unites us in community with the divine:

> [I]n the Will to Interpret, the divine and the human seem to be in closest touch with each other. The mere form of interpretation may be indeed momentarily misused for whatever purpose of passing human folly you will. But if the ideal of interpretation is first grasped; and if then the Community of Interpretation is conceived as inclusive of all individuals; and as unified by the common hope of the far-off event of complete mutual understanding; and, finally, if love for this community is awakened,—then indeed this love is able to grasp, in ideal, the meaning of the Church Universal, of the Communion of Saints, and of God the Interpreter.[4]

In non-Roycean terms, the will to interpret—in its most spiritual manifestation as agapic love—is a radical openness to the possibilities that become imaginable to human persons when they touch the eternal and recognize their dependence on the well-being of others for their own well-being. Insofar as it is construed as an act of recognition, the will to interpret motivates them to pursue a life of loyalty to the ideal of the Beloved Community.

From their perspective, the ideal of the Beloved Community becomes as real as a toothache in their lives.[5] Due to their recognition that the will to interpret is a real phenomenon, their entire way of being in the world changes so that their ethico-religious awareness of the world becomes their primary way of interpreting everything that happens to them. This shift in their way of being would have them be emotionally, intellectually, and spiritually empathetic with their fellows, for they live in an interrelated community of persons who depend on one another to live well-lived lives, or at least good lives—lives in which they are free to pursue our individual life-plans, which also include helping others live out their life-plans and lessening the detrimental conflicts between persons.[6]

We could describe Royce's metaphysics of community as being a philosophical affirmation of Pauline Christianity and its emphasis on the Body of Christ as a universal agapic community. Royce's synthesis of the one and the many in his metaphysics of community, whether he expresses this synthesis in his early language of finite self-representative selves held together by the Absolute or in his later language of a community of persons animated by the spirit of the Universal Community, is similar to Paul's description of the Body of Christ as a diversity-in-unity: "For as the body is one and has many members, but all the members of that one body, being many, are one body, so also is Christ. For by one Spirit we were all baptized into one body—whether Jews or Greeks, whether slaves or free—and have all been made to drink into one Spirit. For in fact the body is not one member but many."[7]

Royce's interpreter-spirit of the Universal Community is agapic love, immanent in every temporal span and recognizable by finite-minded beings. These minded beings, sensing the desirability of pursuing more inclusive communities of persons and responding to the eternal nightingale's call for a more moral universe, are compelled by the divine allure of the ideal of the Beloved Community to act to actualize the Beloved Community more and more in their daily encounters with other persons and even with non-personal beings. Agapic love, for Royce, is the love described in St. Paul's memorable chapter on "Charity": "Love suffers long and is kind; love does not envy; love does not parade itself, is not puffed up; does not behave rudely, does not seek its own, is not provoked, thinks no evil; does not rejoice in iniquity, but rejoices in the truth; bears all things, believes all things, hopes all things, endures all things. Love never fails."[8]

Indeed, *The Problem of Christianity* is Royce's attempt to reinterpret the essential spiritual truths of Christianity in the language of his contemporaries. There Royce exposes the essential spirit of Christianity by transcending any particular cultural and historical events that constitute the Judeo-Christian tradition.[9] He did so in two practical maxims. His first maxim is: "Simplify your Christology."[10] His second practical maxim is: Let your life be guided by the Ideal of the Beloved Community.

> Love this faith, teach this faith, preach this faith, in whatever words, through whatever symbols, by means of whatever forms of creeds, in accordance with whatever practices . . . you find to enable you with a sincere intent and a whole heart to symbolize and to realize the presence of the Spirit of the Community.[11]

Royce goes a step further in his spiritual universalism when he says,

> The core of the faith is the Spirit, the Beloved Community, the work of grace, the atoning deed, and the saving power of the loyal life. There is nothing else under heaven whereby men have been saved or can be saved. To say this is to found no new faith, but to send you to the heart of all true faith.[12]

Royce's metaphysics of community does not only have an ethical and religious dimension to it; it also involves a reinterpretation of scientific inquiry. According to Royce we are fit to interpret our environment in creative and novel ways and to make reliable scientific hypotheses that enable us to live in a precarious and evolving world. The universe is intelligible to us as minded beings, but we do not have the capacity to interpret completely the complex relations between signs that constitute our universe.[13] We only interpret approximately the unity of truth, that is, the Real, using empirical scientific methods and evolutionary theory.[14]

I would be remiss if I ended this section without conveying Royce's portrait of the Logos-Spirit as "servant of all and chief among all."[15] Royce provides an excellent portrait of the Logos-Spirit in terms of being an All-Servant in the following excerpt of *The Problem of Christianity*:

> In such an interpreter [that is, one who interprets all to all, and each individual to the world, and the world of spirits to each individual], and in his community, the problem of the One and the Many would find its ideally complete expression and solution. The abstract conceptions and the mystical intuitions would be at once transcended, and illumined, and yet retained and kept clear and distinct, in and through the life of one who, as interpreter, was at once servant to all and chief among all, expressing his will through all, yet, in his interpretations, regarding and loving the will of the least of these his brethren. In him the Community, the Individual, and the Absolute would be completely expressed, reconciled, and distinguished.[16]

This all-servant is the one who enables us to live in genuine communities. In short, the Logos-Spirit is a person; in fact, the Logos-Spirit fits the profile for what many would call the divine person.

Unlike every other person, the divine person experiences the totality of our universe—past, present, and future—as a concrete fact. As such, the divine person preserves a dynamic, vibrant relationship between actual experiences and possible experiences (at least from the perspective of finite minded beings). This person interprets all reality so that everything is an expression of an overarching totality; yet he conserves the irreducible uniqueness of every finite being while doing so. Oppenheim masterfully describes the nature of Royce's Logos-Spirit in the Epilogue to his *Reverence for the Relations of Life*:

> The Interpreter Spirit mediates, heals, and reconciles alienated individuals and communities. This Spirit calls all authentic loyalists, as well as "lost individuals" [i.e., those individuals who are not considered to be members of any community, and thus alone], to know the risen Christ as Paul did, "not mainly after the flesh, but after the Spirit." By doing so, they can come to recognize him as

the Logos-Spirit, the divine Word who breathes the Spirit of life, light, love, and liberty to both lost and redeemed individuals and communities.[17]

The divine person, then, is the one who "inspires, guides, and empowers"[18] human persons to live lives in accord with the ideal of the Beloved Community.

Royce's 1915–16 Extension Course on Ethics

While Royce's *The Problem of Christianity* can be interpreted as his reply to Howison's criticism on the level of divine personality, his *1915–16 Extension Course on Ethics* furthers his attempt to avoid reducing human personhood to a mode of the divine, as Howison accused him of doing, and to deal with human life in its concreteness and existential complexity. His focus on the human person in his late philosophy should solidify his status as an American personalist, even though we have yet to determine what type of personalist—other than an idealistic one—he is. We shall leave that task for the last chapter. For now, let us examine Royce's late conception of human "person."

For Royce, a human person[19] is an embodied minded being, as Peirce would say. The identity of such a being extends beyond its immediate spatio-temporal participation in the world (i.e., personal existence as present, immediately done activity) or its biochemical and physiological existence (i.e., its actual, brute physicality). A person's identity is constituted by his or her self-conscious pursuit of a particular life-plan, with his or her accompanying life commitments; life projects; memories of past deeds; and anticipations for the future, concerns, and worldview. Moreover, a human person's identity is communal in nature, given that every human cannot develop an identity apart from being a member of numerous communities throughout his or her lifetime. In fact, for a human person to possess a genuine communal identity, and thus a genuine "communal" consciousness, that person must *identify* with the community's past events and deeds as well as *identify* with the future goals that the community desires to actualize. Or, in the case with children and incompetent adults, they have to be recognized by the fully self-conscious members of a community as fellow community members.

Yet, in Royce's thought a group of persons can also constitute a single communal person when they all identify themselves as members of a community with a memory of past events that each member accepts as his or her own past and with an anticipation of a future that each member accepts as a worthy ideal or ideals to actualize as a group and in his or her individual life. No communal person absorbs its constitutive human members into some undifferentiated unity. Instead, we should think of a communal person as a locus of experience where all of its constitutive parts, i.e., its human members, remain distinct, yet united by their shared communal bonds.[20] We could describe the structure of a communal person using this analogy:

A rope is a rope because a group of cords is wound together. Each cord is distinct from every other cord, with its own unique characteristics and identity. However, when any cord becomes interwoven with other cords in the creation of a rope, its primary function becomes to serve as a part of the rope. Despite being part of the rope, each cord retains its identity as a cord, but its identity is expanded to include being part of a larger community of cords, where each cord contributes to the continued existence of the rope and may even contribute to the rope's becoming stronger and more durable. Without each cord of the rope being where it is meant to be the entire rope loses its structural integrity, and if too many cords are either missing or weakened the rope disintegrates.

Royce's human person, accordingly, is simultaneously a communal and individual self. In our living out a life-plan intertwined in communities with others, we interpret ourselves in relation to some past commitments we have agreed to actualize or to our memories of prior events. We also interpret ourselves in relation to what future projects and ideals we want to or decide to pursue in the future. (Of course, we know that sometimes we choose to pursue certain life projects because we feel obligated to do them and not because we want to do them. I believe that this phenomenon is so prevalent in our experience that I do not have to illustrate any examples of it.) We see ourselves as the continual progression toward the actualization of our life-plan, or the continued failure to actualize our life-plan. We not only identify ourselves by our biochemical and physiological attributes, but also by the acts we perform in the world. In the process, we include our habitual use of certain technological artifacts as part of ourselves.

An excellent example of this phenomenon is the way master chefs honor their professional cooking utensils, especially their knives. These chefs often carry their cooking utensils in specially designed attaché cases. When they cook, their knives seem to be an extension of their hands—slicing, dicing, flaying, and quartering food. Another, more ancient example of this phenomenon is the Japanese samurai, whom Royce often refers to in *The Philosophy of Loyalty* and in *The Problem of Christianity*. The samurai's sword is an extension of himself in the world. He and his sword act as one, as he wields his deadly weapon like a blade-shaped limb. He swings his sword like he swings his fist or positions the sword in a defensive stance like he positions his arm in a defensive stance. Both with the chef and the samurai, we see that our self-identity is at least partially determined by what we do.

Nevertheless, we as persons do not have a genuine personal identity outside of being a member of a community. For example, the samurai could not have been a samurai without being inculcated in an ancient Japanese culture where being a samurai was an available, or at least imaginable, way of life for someone to live. This reminds us that we are essentially social beings. Coupled with Royce's appropriation of Peirce's semeiotics,[21] Royce formulates an ethics of responsibility,[22] wherein his late ethics merges with his late metaphysics of community. Oppenheim describes it:

> One knows one's own life-plan by interpretively grasping one's "triplicity of present, past, and future selves," each responsive to the other two. Moreover, one lives socially as "a being who responds to communication with companions". . . . So, unless one

both interpretively knows one's life-plan and interpretively responds to others in society, one cannot generate an intelligent accounting to oneself of one's choices—i.e., be responsible.

Then, too, all of the triads needed for ethical life require truth-seeking interpretations. Royce's most basic triad of sign-sender, sign-receiver, and sign-interpreter realizes itself in the subordinate Roycean triads: (a) of object, believer, and interpreter; (b) of dialogue-partner, self, and interpreter; (c) of past, present, and future selves; and (d) of many other communities of interpretation. . . . But all these triads demand truth-seeking in their interpreters under pain of being irresponsible.[23]

In *Royce's Mature Ethics*, Oppenheim masterfully relates Royce's late metaphysics of community to his ethics, even more so when he discusses the relation between Royce's late epistemology and his metaphysics of community. We can appreciate this excerpt from the preface of Oppenheim's *Royce's Mature Ethics* as a successful effort to unify Royce's late metaphysics of community with his ethics:

During this period, Royce employed an epistemology of interpretation for his ethical reflections. It presupposed a community of embodied "minded beings". . . . [The] ethical life [of those in the community is] to be energized (and in part guided) by the community-members' moral will to interpret and be interpreted. It [is] guided still more by the interpreter-spirit of each community, and indeed by as many of such spirits as there [are] greater, hierarchically arranged communities receiving their direction from the overall Universal Community and its Spirit. In this context, then, Royce's mature ethics call[s] each human self to discern the "eternal" present in its practical here-and-now choice, in its current "mode of moral action." This means "seeing" the Chinese Tao and "touching" it.[24]

Additionally, Royce's *1915–16 Extension Course on Ethics* establishes that Royce did discuss the situatedness of human moral experience in concrete terms. He first establishes that our sense of duty in lived moral experience is not a Kantian duty. Duty "arises, not primarily from pure practical reason, but from concretely lived experiences of the past, once they are recognized as irrevocable."[25] For Royce, then, "duty" is not an abstract, impartial sense of obligation to some moral categorical imperative; it is a sense of obligation we recognize after we reflect upon our past experiences and on whether we lived up to our commitments to others and to the will to interpret in our daily lives. Royce, then, says that the moral philosopher should include all aspects of human existence—for example, bodily states, human evils, human goods—"especially the basic ones of life and death, as these affect both body and moral self" in their moral philosophy.[26] Royce also admonishes us that any moral philosophy that ignores the network of embodied, minded selves in its bondedness to nature, fortune, societies, and God is "a mere abstraction."[27] Additionally, our moral experience involves analyzing the paradoxes arising out of the interaction between us, our environment, our society, our socioeconomic status, and God, and being faithful to this paradoxical element of our moral experience in our description of it.[28] Finally, Royce acknowledges that religious sentiment is always permeating our moral experience, and thus should have a prominent role in any ethical theory.[29]

In his *Extension Course on Ethics*, Royce explicitly describes the role of embodiedness in human experience, especially in our moral experience. This course is also where Royce's personalism crystallizes its ethics. True to his allegiance to a Jamesian psychology, Royce would say that prior to any intellectual conception about human cognition or any metaphysical description of reality we experience the world personally. That is, before we are "rational animals" or "modes of an Infinite Self" or "Leibnizian monads" or "highly evolved organisms with self-referential cognition," we think; we feel; we love; we yearn; we emote; we live. All this is the personal mode of experiencing the world manifesting itself socially. Furthermore, since we experience ourselves and the world personally, our primary mode of being-in-the-world is *Mitsein*; we are never atomic monads, metaphysically independent, but essentially social beings, for to be a personal being is to always already be born and live in community with other persons. Even the adult human person who decides to live apart from other human persons could not have become conscious of himself as a hermit without first living in a community of human persons. And even after he leaves human society to live alone, he lives in a natural community with non-human animals. He is always dependent on other selves, whether human or non-human, for his existence. This is an undeniable fact, if not *the* undeniable fact, of human existence.

Royce's late ethics also depends on his tripartite analysis of human personhood. Oppenheim gives us a concise summary:

> Royce viewed the human person phenomenologically as an historical process whose chosen plan of life gives [her or him] unity and self-identity. Metaphysically, the human person is an embodied minded being interacting in community. Ethically Royce saw the human person as a living reality called to transmute its individualistic self-identity by devoting oneself to the cause of some genuine community.... Persons remain in their roots mysteries never fully to be comprehended by finite minded beings. In the end, then, they can be "fairly understood" only if interpreted through at least a pair of approaches: one as unique individual, the other as community; one as real interpreter, the other as sign to be interpreted communally.[30]

As the above excerpt demonstrates, Royce thinks of the human person as simultaneously being a phenomenological self, a metaphysical self, and an ethical self. As a phenomenological self, a human person experiences herself as a felt, lived historical process unified through her acts of living according to a certain form of life.[31] As a metaphysical self, a human person experiences herself as an embodied minded being that is dependent on a divine whole and on other finite beings to existence. As an ethical self, a human person should live in such ways that she pursues "the invisible community of humankind's shared spiritual interests, ideals, and hopes and of its shared processes of communication and cooperation."[32] Furthermore, this pursuit should manifest itself, to a certain extent, in all daily interpersonal encounters. Otherwise, one is not being an adequately ethical self.

Despite these descriptive distinctions in Royce's analysis, no one could postulate a "clear and distinct" ontological distinction among these three aspects of human existence without being unfaithful to our experience. This means that I as a human self experience myself as a phenomenological-ethico-religious being. I have *felt*, or *lived*, experiences of myself and of others in an environing world. I am also aware of some transcendent Beyond where all beings are held together within himself. I am, thirdly, a member of many directly interrelated and indirectly related communities of interpretation which, ideally, should strive to better approximate the Ideal of the Beloved Community.

In Royce's late philosophy, then, Royce embraces the philosophical thesis that our lived experience, in our lived body (as Merleau-Ponty would say), is the existential starting-point for all intellectual inquiries, especially into the nature of human morality. This makes Royce's late thought similar to Jamesian and Peircean pragmatisms—with their emphasis on lived life and the experience of existential doubt as the beginning of philosophical inquiry. It is especially similar to Jamesian pragmatism for another reason—with its contention that one's philosophy is reflective of one's essential personal temperament, refined in the process of philosophical inquiry.

Finally, this gives Royce's answer to Howison's question: How could he preserve the individuality of human persons within an ethico-religious Whole maintained by the Absolute, or Interpreter Spirit of the Beloved Community? We are dependent on the Absolute, or the divine, for our existence, yet we still have the freedom to choose our form of life and by living out that form of life in our daily embodied existence we contribute to the divine will and to the Universal Community.

A Comparison of Royce's and Howison's Idealisms

I hope it is obvious to the reader that Royce's late idealism does answer Howison's major criticism of his earlier idealism. Yet, Royce's late idealism is not only an answer to Howison's idealistic criticism of his earlier "absolute" idealism. Some would even say that Royce's metaphysics of community is similar to Howison's City of God.[33] And there is some truth to that contention. The similarities between Royce's idealism and Howison's idealism go further, though. For example, neither Royce nor Howison thinks that Darwinian evolutionary theory could exhaustively explain our world or us as embodied minded beings or intelligent organisms.

Royce and Howison are also similar in that their conceptions of God suffer from the same philosophical weakness: there is an insufficient explanation (in Howison's case, no explanation) of how God functions as the creator of life, including us embodied minded beings, and they, therefore, do not sufficiently portray God's full actuality, or God as *esse in re*. Royce does come closer to discussing God as *esse in re* than Howison. At least Royce's God is the ultimate preserver of embodied beings and the ontological ground out of which they emerge and acts only insofar as embodied beings, especially embodied minded beings, act in the world.

Another point of similarity between Royce and Howison is that they both think that we are capable of recognizing our duty to live up to our status as members of an eternal community of persons— whether that community is called the City of God (Howison) or the ever-distant-yet-near Beloved Community (Royce). At the very least, we human organisms have the active capacity or the potential to recognize such a duty to live in that way. Our spiritual and ethical lives transcend any empirical scientific theories of nature.

Royce would say that such an ethico-religious awareness should bring us to be mindful that we live in a value-laden and meaning-rich world, an axiological realm, with our scientific descriptions of natural processes and ourselves being significant only insofar as these descriptions enable us to accomplish certain tasks, commune with nature, live an enriching life, or help our fellow person. In other words, scientific, or "objective," descriptions of reality are significant only if they assist us in living life more fully and beneficially. And we can see that Royce considers life to be well lived wherever there are persons who act out of a spirit of "loyalty to loyalty" or the Spirit of the Universal Community.

Howison has a similar metaphysics of community, where God serves as the Ideal of the City of God. All finite persons "harmonize" their conduct and their ideals to better commune with God as fellow, co-eternal members of the City of God.[34] All finite persons who recognize and are compelled by the divine ideal gravitate toward it, like the planets revolve around the sun. These finite persons are eternal to the extent that they act in accordance with the divine ideal. Eternity is the everlastingness of the divine ideal, that is, whether persons have acted on it in the past, act on it now, or will act on it in the future, it remains the same, beyond time, beyond change.

In nineteenth-century German idealistic terms, Howison's God is a Kantian philosophical deity, real only as an ideal, as the unchanging eternal ideal we rational moral agents yearn to commune with in a community beyond the boundaries of temporal processes. Moreover, we as rational, moral agents are eternal insofar as we commune with one another in the spirit of this ideal. This why Howison defines "eternity" this way:

> [E]ternity, or free reality, means something quite transcending [the "everlastingness," or the indestructible, perpetual continuance of the futurity, that is "a real *aspect* in the being of ... free self-consciousness"]. It means that each thoroughly real being is just self-defining, self-operative, is existent in a sense that excludes the alternatives of its non-existence—its central unifying essence is quite out of and independent of time, or is *necessary* (*i.e.,* unavoidable and necessitating) instead of necessitated; and that, in fact, *time itself takes its rise entirely from this self-thinking which constitutes the free being as eternal and whole.*[35]

Time, then, is derivative of the spontaneous activity of our acting according to the eternal moral ideal that is God.[36] God, in turn, is real only as a spiritual being, a timeless being, and we can commune with God only as spirits. Howison equates spirit with pure practical reason manifesting itself in its acting according to the categorical imperative, especially as it is expressed in Kant's practical imperative: "So act as to treat humanity, whether in thine own person or in that of any other, in every case as an end withal, never as means only."[37]

Royce would agree with Howison that God and the most essential part of us is spirit. For Royce, however, God is also the ontological ground for temporality itself and, while transcending any particular time span, is immanent in every moment of time along with being an Ideal. In Royce's late philosophy, the divine will is (a) the Infinite Person who "remembers" the past by preserving all prior occurrences in the universe within itself, (b) the perpetual fellow-sufferer in the present, uniting all existent beings within itself (i.e., being immanent in the world) and giving us access to the past in the present via the Will to Interpret, and (c) the Ideal of the Beloved Community.

Concerning human persons, Royce thinks that we live spiritually to the extent that we transcend our immediate sense impressions and carnal yearnings and actively participate in the partial actualization of the Beloved Community. Howison would agree with Royce thus far. But Royce takes his spirituality a step further. Unlike Howison, he thinks that we can even participate spiritually in the emergence of the Beloved Community on earth after we die a biological death since we live on not only in the memory of those we encountered while we were alive, but also because all of our deeds are forever an objective part of the universe. In a way, we are immortal to the extent that we still have an effect on living persons and on the one who remembers all once we have died.[38] Royce even lived out his faith in objective immortality by honoring his departed loved ones and his philosophical predecessors in what he called a "cult of the dead." What is telling about Royce's "cult of the dead" is that he valued this community of departed spirit until his dying day.[39]

When Royce's late philosophy is compared with Howison's personal idealism, Royce is easily identifiable as a personalist, but not quite a Howisonian personalist in the sense Rufus Burrow, Jr.'s defines Howisonian personalism in *Personalism: A Critical Introduction*[40] nor in the sense of Howison's personal idealism as defined in Chapter 1 and in this section. As we have seen above, Royce's personalism is more existential and experiential than Howison's. Furthermore, Royce's personalism better accounts for the origin and existence of the plurality of selves and persons than does Howison's personal idealism. Indeed Howison thought that the essence of all selves worthy of the name "person" is uncreated and acted upon when they "aspire toward God."[41]

What sort of personalist is Royce, then? Is his personalism compatible with the Boston personalist tradition? Once one no longer reads Royce as a nineteenth-century absolute idealist, that question becomes an interesting one and will be the primary focus of the next chapter.

FOUR

ROYCE'S PERSONALISM

Is Josiah Royce's personalism compatible with the Boston personalist tradition? We already know that Royce is unquestionably a personalist because he accepts the central descriptive hypotheses of personalism. These are, according to *The Personalist Forum*, formerly the official organ of contemporary American personalism: (1) "it is the personal dimension of our being and living that is definitive of our humanity"[1] and (2) "the personal dimension of being-human offers a clue to the ordering of reality."[2] Royce is also a personalist because his philosophy embodies Erazim Kohak's articulation of personalism:

> Personalism is a philosophy predicated upon the irreducibility and primacy of personal categories, that is, the kind of categories that govern the meaningful interaction among personal beings—categories of meaning rather than cause, of respect rather than force, of moral value rather than efficacy, of understanding rather than explanation. While [personalists] recognize the legitimacy of materialistic categories derived from the metaphor of matter in

motion and of vitalistic categories derived from the metaphor of need and satisfaction for certain purposes, [personalists] regard them as derivative, special case theories legitimate within the basic framework of personal categories. It is moral categories that [personalists] consider epistemologically and ontologically fundamental, not merely a peculiarity of human subjects but most approximating the ultimate structure of reality. In a time honored metaphor, though reality can at times be treated as a system of matter in motion, ultimately it is a *society of persons*, and is so to be understood.[3]

As we have demonstrated in the preceding chapters, Royce's late philosophy is a personalism in Kohak's sense of personalism, and, with Kohak's affiliation with Boston University and his familiarity with the Bostonian personalist tradition, we could then say that Royce's idealistic personalism has some affinity with Boston personalism.[4] Both would agree that

> [w]hat personalism does mean is that we can not only interpret, but experience reality in a personalistic posture, as structured primordially by subject-related categories of value and meaning. . . . the personalist recognition is that primary meaning relationships are [person-*al*], not impersonal, that humans are not the only person-*al* beings and that the person-*al* is not private and arbitrary.[5]

One could question my association of Royce's philosophy with personalism, however. It is well-known that Royce, particularly in *The Problem of Christianity*, contends that there are two levels of personhood: (1) individual human persons and (2) communal persons consisting of individual human persons in community with one another. I state as much in the last chapter. He also contends that communal persons are more significant and even more real than individual persons. He asserts the truth of the above-mentioned contention as follows: "The communities are vastly more complex, and, in many ways, are also immeasurably more potent and enduring than are the individuals."[6] Here is where Royce's two-level theory of personhood becomes problematic for many of his critics. They would object to Royce's conception of personhood by asking such questions as these: How is a communal person personal? Are not only individual human persons *personal*?

Royce could easily answer these questions in a manner that solidifies his connection to personalism, as defined by Kohak. He could say that the presuppositions behind the objectors' questions are wrong. That is, the objectors are wrong to presuppose that personal equals private. This is to reduce personal categories to the realm of private fancy and individual consciousness. As we have seen, Royce's entire philosophy is a rejection of that very presupposition. For Royce, a communal person can be just as personal as an individual human person; moreover, personal categories, for example, personality, loyalty, good, and evil, are applicable to communal persons as well as individual human persons.[7] In fact, the consciousness (or, as Royce calls it, "mental existence") of communal persons are, "in general, far more potent and, for certain purposes and in certain activities, much more intelligent than are the human individuals whose separate physical organisms we ordinarily regard as signs of so many separate minds."[8] We can also contend, following Royce, that communal persons are not empirical objects that can be understood via scientific categories alone. In short, communal persons are more than just natural entities; they are also spiritual members of the Beloved Community.

As more significant members of the Beloved Community than any single human person, communal persons are often more responsive to divine grace than any individual human person would be. That is so because communal persons are the organs for divine grace to affect the individual human members of that person.[9] They are the "bodies" in which "the individual [human person] obtains, for his ideally extended self, precisely the unity, the wealth, and the harmony of plan which his sundered natural [i.e., empirical] existence never supplies."[10]

All in all, then, I think that the above description of communal persons does not disqualify Royce from being considered a personalist. What it does is expand Kohak's statement, "though reality can at times be treated as a system of matter in motion, ultimately it is a society of persons, and is so to be understood,"[11] to include communities as persons in their own right within the society of persons.

At this point, an important question arises: How do I account for Borden Parker Bowne's criticism of Royce's supposed absolute idealism if Royce is indeed a personalist who embodies many of the characteristics of Boston personalism? Bowne's criticism of Josiah Royce's idealism is similar to Howison's 1895 criticism of Royce's idealism. Like Howison, Bowne thought that Royce's personalism was a personalistic absolutism, where persons are only modes of the Absolute. Accordingly, Bowne—a staunch opponent of idealistic absolutism—had a serious problem with such a personalistic absolutism because it destroys the individuality of God and profanes the divine in the process. Burrow, quoting Bowne, gives Bowne's criticism of personalistic absolutism:

> It is no doubt fine, and in some sense it is correct, to say that God is in all things; but when it comes to saying that God is all things and that all forms of thought and feeling and conduct are his, then reason simply commits suicide. God thinks and feels in what we call our thinking and feeling; and hence he blunders in our blundering and is stupid in our stupidity. He contradicts himself also with the utmost freedom; for a [good] deal of his thinking does not hang together from one person to another, or from one day to another in the same person. Error, folly, and sin are all made divine; and reason and conscience as having authority vanish. The only thing that is not divine in this scheme is God.[12]

Given the novelty of Royce's "*relational form* of the ontological argument"[13] for God's existence, one can understand why Bowne criticizes Royce's idealism the way he did. He, along with Howison, did not have the advantage of critical distance to evaluate Royce's late idealism as a proto-process philosophy. He mistakenly equated Royce's idealism with pantheism even though it was actually panentheistic. Besides, Royce did not offer a comprehensive articulation of his metaphysical personalism until 1913, with the publication of *The Problem of Christianity*, a few years after Bowne's death. Moreover,

Royce's contemporaries were too familiar with his earlier work to appreciate the gradual, yet profound, shift in his thought.[14]

Burrow has the critical distance to interpret Royce's philosophy, particularly Royce's writings during and after 1908, in a more favorable light than Bowne did or even could, but he still interprets Royce's idealism as a personalistic absolutism. Yet, Burrow's affirmation of the African expression—"I am, because we are; and since we are, therefore I am"—and the sociality central to such an understanding of our personhood complements Royce's late conception of the human person. Royce and Burrow would agree that every person is an irreducibly distinct embodied being, while simultaneously being dependent on other persons (and non-personal, cosmic processes that we encounter personally) to live and foster the relationships essential for him or her to become a mature person. This has been Royce's position all along; he never thought that our individuality is "swallowed up" by any Absolute. Indeed, Royce's personalism is a panentheistic interpretation of 1 John 4:13 (NIV): "We know that we live in [God] and he in us, because he has given us of his Spirit."

Actually, Royce has a more comprehensive metaphysics than Howison or Burrow. Unlike Howison, Royce distinguishes between our metaphysical dependence on something beyond ourselves to exist at all (i.e., God as the ontological ground of being) and the ideal nature of God. Unlike Bowne and Burrow, Royce considers God as the preserver of previous events done by once-living persons and non-minded beings within the present and carries all of these objectified relations into the future. Royce holds onto the conception that unity is always already an interconnected matrix of relations among many phenomena. That is, unity is always a plurality-in-unity for Royce.

Furthermore, Royce's pluralistic monism, like Howison's personal idealism and Boston personalism, argues against the Hegelian Absolute. It does so because the Hegelian Absolute, at least as it is portrayed in Hegel's later writings (for example, *Philosophy of Right*), ceases to be a genuine person and swallows up and forgets any historical particularity that does not assist it in advancing toward complete self-consciousness. Royce's Absolute, and later his Interpreter Spirit, remembers all historical particularities within himself and is what he is only because of these particularities interacting with one another, ideally, in the spirit of the Beloved Community. This notion of the Absolute as agapic love is vastly different than Hegel's Absolute and more similar to Howison's God and even to the traditional Christian belief that God is Love.

Said in another way, Royce's personalism claims that we are simultaneously in God, of God, expressing God's will on earth, and distinct from God in every sense except in a temporal and ethico-religious sense. Because Royce's divine is Temporality itself,[15] or the condition for temporal beings to exist at all, and insofar as we personal beings relate to one another in time, we relate to a personal God who exists in time, yet beyond any specific time-span.

For Royce, we could not relate to the world or to God in any other way than as personal beings who interpret ourselves and our world via personal modes of existence—for example, concern, curiosity, or anticipation. Furthermore, the way we interpret ourselves and the world influences how we treat ourselves, one another, and the ecosystem.

Essentially, if we interpret the world as an impersonal universe, then we tend to see ourselves and everything else in mechanistic terms, as interchangeable parts in a vast, cold universe. At most, in such an interpretation of reality, we project meaning onto the universe, realizing that we have no significance beyond whatever significance we attach to ourselves at any particular moment. We are left to human caprice to determine our life's meaning.

Royce, in contrast, would say that we should interpret reality as a community of persons, striving for the actualization of the Universal Community in which all persons remain themselves while contributing to the welfare of others. With the inhumanity of World War I occurring in the final years of Royce's life, and despite the fact that he sometimes aligned himself with regional loyalties (i.e., the Allied Powers) along with loyalty to the Beloved Community in these last years, Royce held fast to his personalistic idealism and its personal interpretation of reality.

Royce agrees with the Boston personalists such as Edgar S. Brightman and Peter A. Bertocci, that every human person

> is a complex unity, a *unitas multiplex*.... All of the complex data of any particular conscious being belong together in a unique way; "my" experience is mine only and cannot be handed over to anyone else. Not only do the present data hang together uniquely, but they are also connected uniquely with past and future data by linkages of memory and of anticipation.... The whole self is the whole range of present, past, and future experiences that belong with a datum self [i.e., a present complex consciousness] by virtue of conscious linkages.[16]

So they all agree that without such a unity of the human self we could not have any faithful account of ourselves as moral beings.

We might also note that Royce's personalism, according to Burrow's classification, is a more "thoroughgoing, typical personalist" than most scholars have initially thought. In fact, Royce's late personalism is at least as typical as Howison's teleological or ethical personalism. When comparing Royce's personalism to the central traits of "thoroughgoing, typical" Boston personalism, Royce affirms eight of the ten traits of Bostonian personalism, affirms another one of these traits with some reservations, and only rejects one of the ten traits outright. The eight traits that Royce's personalism affirms with Boston personalists are (1) the centrality of persons, both metaphysically and ethically; (2) a "fundamentally and thoroughly idealistic" philosophy;[17] (3) theistic; (4) "freedomistic;"[18] (5) a coherence criterion of truth (i.e., a fallibilist notion of truth where all belief-systems are subject to alteration depending on the most recent available knowledge of the world and not a static correspondence theory of truth where we attempt to have our ideas merely "correspond" to some state of affairs independent of ourselves); (6) a "synoptic-analytic method";[19] (7) the central philosophical thesis that "reality is through and through social or relational;"[20] and (8) that any viable philosophy should be a radically empirical one, since that sort of philosophy appears to be most faithful to our lived experience.

The trait where Royce's personalism agrees with Boston personalists but with moderate reservations is a creationist account of the universe. Royce would agree with Boston personalists that God functions as the World-ground in which beings live and have their being, but he does not concentrate on God as Creator, but on God as ontological preserver of temporality and as ideal of the Beloved Community. He does not explicitly say that God created the world *ex nihilo*, and he generally neglected to describe how God can create finite beings. Yet, Royce does not claim that persons are *causa sui*, as Howison's personalism would.[21]

The only trait of Boston personalism that Royce definitely would reject in his personalism is a "personalistic epistemology [that] is activistic and dualistic."[22] Royce would tend to agree with Burrow and other Boston personalists that in an activistic epistemology "mind is not just the Lockean passive *tabula rasa* or blank slate on which data are written. Instead, the mind receives or takes in data, for example, sensations, but it is also active and creative. The mind acts on what is taken in."[23]

However, Royce would disagree with the notion of a dualistic mind-object relation "in the sense that my idea of an object and the object itself are not completely identical, although there is a relation between them."[24] He would contend that such a dualistic epistemology is too simplistic to account for our acquisition of knowledge. Rather, Royce offers a triadic interpretative epistemology where the most basic unit of knowledge is not mind-object but an interpretative act between minded beings consisting of a sign to be interpreted by someone, an interpreter of that sign, and a minded being who receives the interpreter's analysis and expression of that sign's meaning. In fact, in any act of interpretation, the same embodied minded being may be an interpreter of a sign referring to some past event and the very one who receives the interpreter's interpretation of the past sign in the present or future. Indeed, these intrapersonal interpretative acts are how we acquire both self-knowledge and knowledge of the external world. Griffin Trotter gives an excellent example of Royce's epistemology on an intrapersonal and then an interpersonal level:

Suppose I wake up at 4 A.M. to go to the bathroom, and, as I traverse the dark hallway, I experience a searing sensation in my left foot. This sensation, in the instant it occurs, is relatively unreflective: it occurs abruptly and was unanticipated, and it is intense, so that it pushes other aspects of thought beyond the periphery of consciousness. Let us designate this instant as T1 (Thought-Sign #1). In the very next instant, the searing sensation, which may already be decreasing in intensity, becomes the object of interpretation. That is, T1 becomes an object for interpretation in T2. I might exclaim, "Ouch," and in so doing I interpret T1 as an experience of pain. My exclamation at T2 (even if my "ouch" were non-verbal) is "aimed" at succeeding thoughts—its interpretants. I am saying that I have experienced pain. In this case the message is relayed without deliberation, out of habit, but it is a message nonetheless. It establishes continuity between my present state and the states that precede and succeed it. Terms like *ouch* and concepts [percepts?] such as pain are reinforced because they are useful. The information they relay to future states of the self, and to other persons, will be utilized to make decisions.

The interpretation of T1 may be further refined. The T1–T2 complex can be taken as a sign in itself, and might be interpreted at T3 with the thought, "I've hurt my foot once again on one of Shane's toys." T3, of course, could factor into a whole string of eventual interpretations, for instance (Tx) my decision to bar Shane from playing Nintendo until he quits leaving his GI Joes lying in the hallway, (Ty) my wife's decision, when I return to bed, to hold off on asking me for a back rub, and (Tz) Shane's observation that the essence of virtue is to avoid being messy.[25]

See how a single instance where a guy who stubs his toe on his son's toy serves as an interpretative sign for a variety of interpreters, with this sign having multiple meanings depending on who interprets it. His wife could interpret that event as the reason to postpone her request for a back rub until he feels better. His son could interpret the same event as a reason not to leave his toys in the hallway. The husband himself could interpret this event not only as an occasion to punish his son for leaving toys in the hallway, but also to become more mindful of what might be on the floor the next time he walks in the hallway at night or to turn the hallway light on whenever he ventures out into the hallway at night. This single event demonstrates how a mind-object epistemology reduces the complexity of our lived experience into an artificial mind-object relation. Unlike a dualistic epistemology, a triadic epistemology does not posit the existence of a mind-independent object or state of affairs that we actively appropriate within ourselves via *a priori* categories, as in Kantian epistemology, for simplicity's sake.

A Roycean triadic epistemology affirms, first and foremost, that any object of knowledge has meaning only insofar as is recognized by some minded being in a particular context; that is, someone has to interpret an object as expressing a meaning before we can conduct an inquiry into its epistemic meaning in a given circumstance. We cannot know anything about an object beyond our capacity to interpret its meaning(s) from a given interpretative perspective. In other words, a triadic epistemology is even more "mindful" than a dualistic epistemology, even an activistic one, because it reminds us that we cannot speak of anything intelligibly unless that thing is already recognized as being meaningful to someone, in some specific context.

Moreover, Royce's triadic epistemology would contend that the real—that is, the totality of all prior existent and current existent beings with all their potentialities (along with possibilities divorced from any actual state of affairs in the world)—is accessible to us only because some transhistorical cosmic process, or Interpreter Spirit, perpetually interprets it and weaves together all beings, with their expressions of meanings, into a single, unified matrix of meanings. These perpetual interpretative acts of the Interpreter Spirit have a tendency of favoring expressions of meanings that advance the expansion of agapic love in human life. Actually, Boston personalism needs a Roycean interpretative epistemology for its epistemology to be truly radical in its empiricism and improve its fidelity to persons' lived experiences as persons-in-communities.

Royce's entire philosophy could be interpreted as a panentheistic personalism insofar as he affirms both the divine World Spirit as the ground for all being and the moral agency of persons while they are simultaneously dependent on the divine World Spirit for their existence. Accordingly, his personalism is closer to Boston personalism than Howison's teleological personalism is to Boston personalism. Surprisingly, Royce's personalism could be interpreted as a weird synthesis of Howison's personal idealism and Bostonian personalistic idealism.

Consequently, I am tempted to call Royce's personalism an ethical and panentheistic personalism, a personalism that is a philosophical system which pursues knowledge about reality by having knowledge of persons and their means of acquiring knowledge of themselves and their environing world and experiencing the divine. This pursuit of knowledge, via personal categories of existence, enables us to appreciate the most ennobling things we can experience—aesthetic awe, healthy experiencing of eros–philia–agape–familial love, moments of empowering tranquility while being in an ecstatic commune with the Everlasting Eternal, genuine concern for other persons and our environing world, preserving the majesty of nature.

In an unlikely passage from *The Problem of Christianity*, Royce explains the characteristic shared by Roycean personalism, Boston personalism, and Howisonian personal idealism that makes them worthy of philosophical study:

> You are not a mere extension by analogy of my own will to live. I do not, for the sake merely of such analogy, vivify your perceived organism. *You are an example of the principle whose active recognition lies at the basis of my only reasonable view of the universe. As I treat you, so ought I to deal with the universe. As I interpret the universe, so, too, in principle, should I interpret you.*[26]

If Royce is right, then Boston personalism and Howison's personal idealism still has some philosophical viability. If I interpret the cosmos as a thoroughly impersonal process in which we are merely the latest organism emerging from an evolutionary process, devoid of any purpose, of any intentionality, and wherein life itself was a cosmic accident, then it is difficult, if not impossible, to justify treating anyone outside of my religion, my ethnicity, or my geopolitical region with dignity and respect. World War I, World War II, the Holocaust, and the more recent acts of genocide in Bosnia-Herzegovina, Kosovo, and Rwanda are evidence of the difficulty of respecting human personhood in an impersonal age prone to reducing humanity to human resources, interchangeable commodities, consumers, and producers of goods, or to sick, perverted beasts with advanced intelligence.

Naturalistic humanism—in the non-reductive materialist tradition of Ralph Barton Perry, George Santayana, John Dewey, John Herman Randall, Jr., and John Ryder—attempts to preserve the dignity of human persons by respecting their emergence from evolutionary processes and the richness of our relations to one another and our ecosystem. However, they do not sufficiently emphasize that the cosmos is not only amiable to our survival, and sometimes even to our well being, but also personally responsive and receptive to our ethical, aesthetic, and religious efforts to live meaningful lives. Interpreting the universe as being personal and responsive to us—even though our world is a precarious one—would remind us that human personhood is precious and deserves to be respected by persons.

By thinking of the universe as a community of persons, we are more prone to respect persons than by regarding the universe as a cosmic accident. Besides, saying that a non-personal evolutionary process eventually led to the emergence of personal organisms that yearn for a personal cosmos is at least as plausible as saying that our universe is a personal cosmos that responds positively to acts done in the spirit of piety, humility, fallibility, and loyalty to the Beloved Community. On further consideration, given that the universe is, at minimum, *compatible* with personal existence, contending that the universe is personal insofar as it responds positively to acts done in the spirit of piety, humility, generosity, fallibility, and loyalty to the Beloved Community seems more reasonable than contending that the universe is an impersonal one or the result of a cosmic accident.[27]

Indeed, saying that our universe is a personal one is more faithful to our experience as persons-in-community, where our community not only includes other human persons, but also everything else comprising our environing world—for example, non-human persons, non-minded beings, and natural processes such as seasonal climate changes on the earth.

Studying Royce's late philosophy as a form of idealistic personalism leads me to conclude that any contemporary Roycean idealistic personalism would resemble the following portrait of idealism. A Roycean idealistic personalism would no longer deny the facticity of our embodied existence and the plausibility of physcialist interpretations of it (e.g., the human self as interpreted by the natural sciences—biology, chemistry, physics, and neuroscience—and cognitive science, all with their allegiance to scientific realism).

However, a Roycean idealistic personalism does recognize that our lived experience cannot be confined to such physicalist interpretations and explanations of our embodied existence. That is because we sometimes transcend our brute physicality, even though in this life we are always, as far as we know, embodied beings dependent on an organic locus of experience to maintain a coherent identity (or if the technology ever becomes available to have human-like cognitive and precognitive processes located and enacted in a non-organic medium). We are able to transcend our brute physicality by letting our conduct be guided by ideal, yet real and significant, standards. These ideal standards are not simply epiphenomenal or the result of highly developed brains with the capacity for long-term strategic planning and abstract problem-solving. They are the manifestations of our spiritual existence, of our anticipation for the future, of our tendency to act for-the-sake-of-which, in ancient Greek terms and later Heideggerian terms, or in pursuit of an end-in-view, in Deweyan terms. This spiritual existence is a dimension of our lived experience; it is as natural as the wind blowing or the sun shinning or the rain falling. Often these ideal standards are more significant to our lives than our immediate physiological existence.

I would add that we participate in a continual spiritual process where certain ideals, or potentialities, are cognitively grasped and yearned for, are actualized by sentient organisms in cooperation with natural processes, by sentient organisms using technological artifacts to alter our environing world—whether these alterations are beneficial or detrimental to our environing world's long-term health—and through which they accomplish their desired ends, or by natural processes unaided by any sentient organism. This spiritual process is divine, but not all ideal standards are beneficial either for those persons who act on them or for those who suffer the consequences of someone or some community of persons acting on certain ideals. To have a moral and genuinely spiritual process of actualizing ideals and potentialities in the form of events and objects (in the sense of Deweyan events with meaning), we expand our ideal standards to acknowledge the most-inclusive Ideal that demands our loyalty, the Beloved Community.

Furthermore, a contemporary Roycean idealistic personalism is a concrete and even a semi-realistic philosophy because it realizes that we first have to change our interpretation of other persons from an impersonal and/or materialistic one to one in which we regard other persons as fellow members of a larger community of persons such that if anyone suffers or is oppressed, then we all suffer and are oppressed. Therefore, we should do everything within our financial resources and personal power to alleviate such suffering and equip these persons with the means to live at least a decent life. All of this must be accomplished before we have a chance to actually change the oppressive material conditions for the "multitude" of persons living today.

To act ethically involves first regarding other persons beyond one's relatives, friends, acquaintances, lovers, partners, neighbors, etc. as worthy of respect. But to regard others as persons worthy of respect involves respecting their physicality—their bodily integrity and psychological and emotional well being. Of course, this idealistic interpretation of our social conditions is an inversion of the historical materialistic dialectic.

Exemplars of such a contemporary Roycean idealistic personalism are the Boston personalists Martin Luther King, Jr., and Walter Muelder, the prophetic pragmatism of Cornel West, and the militant personalism of Rufus Burrow, Jr.—in short, any personalism or ethical-oriented, person-centered philosophy in which adherents actually confront social and economic injustices in their work.[28] They do not separate their theoretical personalism from praxis; their personalism is a refined second-order articulation and extension of their daily struggles against moral injustice and their daily affirmation of the dignity of all persons.

In many philosophic circles, it is a controversial position to assert that a person who advances a certain philosophical position should live according to it. However, all of these personalists are Socratic philosophers in the sense that philosophy is a way of life for them and not some academic exercise or only an occupation; philosophy is a vocation for these personalists—a way of life. Indeed, these personalisms are persuasive precisely because they are embodied in the lives and actions of those persons who espouse them.

PART TWO

EXTENDING ROYCE'S ETHICO-RELIGIOUS INSIGHT: ROYCE ON THE BELOVED COMMUNITY, *AGAPE*, AND HUMAN TEMPORALITY

FIVE

ROYCE'S ETHICO-RELIGIOUS INSIGHT: A HYPOTHETICAL POSTULATE?

Until now I have dealt with Royce's ethico-religious insight as he articulated it from his 1895 "Conception of God" essay through his *1915–16 Extension Course on Ethics*. I have presumed that Royce's philosophic propositions described features of our reality in an unproblematic way. Given Royce's argumentation and his ethico-religious insight, I contended that he holds a personalistic philosophy where God is fellow sufferer and could be viewed as Temporality itself (or, more accurately, as the One whose temporality is the basis for all other sorts of temporality), and where God is partially an ideal (or more specifically, the ideal of the Beloved Community) that we have the potential to recognize and act upon in our lives.

A notable portion of this chapter consists of a condensed and revised version of the first section of my article "Concerning the God That Is Only a Concept: A Marcellian Critique of Royce's God," *Transactions of the Charles S. Peirce Society: A Quarterly Journal in American Philosophy* 42.3 (Summer 2006): 394–416. Reprinted by permission of Indiana University Press.

What complicates this interpretation of Royce's philosophy is that I have not taken into account Randall Auxier's recent interpretation of Josiah Royce in his encyclopedia entry on Josiah Royce in *Modern Dictionary of American Philosophers*[1] and his paper "Royce's Fictional Ontology,"[2] where he contends that Royce's philosophy is best understood as one constructed out of hypothetical postulates that are deemed adequate only insofar as they are exemplified in our actual experiences of the world. Moreover, these postulates are not limited to generalizations, that is, propositions constructed from our empirical observations of certain phenomena; rather, they may also be universal propositions that we posit in an effort to make sense of our empirical observations of certain phenomena.

What this means is that Royce's philosophic postulates are hypothetical propositions in the sense that they aim to make our empirical observations intelligible. They frame our empirical observations in such a way that they fit into a coherent view of the world. What Royce aims to do in his philosophy is construct a series of interrelated hypothetical postulates that grounds every empirical observation we make or experience we have into a single rational framework. These hypothetical postulates demonstrate their descriptive adequacy to the extent that they are exemplified in our actual experiences of the world.[3]

Yet, the most significant reason that Royce seeks to construct a single rational framework to fit all of our actual (and possible) experiences of the world into is his ethico-religious insight. He thinks that the most adequate description of our world involves regarding it as a single moral system populated by persons who commune with one another and with the divine. In valuing practical reason over theoretical reason in this way, Royce's philosophy is thoroughly Kantian. Indeed, he began his philosophic career by announcing that one of the things Kant taught subsequent philosophers is that any philosophic system is worthwhile only to the extent that it regards ethics as first philosophy, as he expressed in the closing pages of his 1881 article "Kant's Relation to Modern Philosophic Progress":

> The goal of philosophy can be reached only in an Ethical Doctrine. For since the ultimate fact of the knowing consciousness is

the active construction of a world of truth from the data of sense, the ultimate justification of this activity must be found in the significance—i.e., in the moral worth—of this activity itself, a matter only to be discussed in the light of Ethics.[4]

Given the hypothetical nature of Royce's philosophy, as articulated by Auxier's reading of it, how can I justify my interpretation of Royce's ethico-religious insight in the first part of this book? My interpretation seems to depend upon Royce's philosophic propositions being more than mere postulates; in fact, my interpretation of Royce's philosophy is nonsensical, or at the very least fanciful, unless Royce's philosophic propositions are able to denote actually existing features of our world. Royce seems to have the same intuition as I do. For example, in his *The Religious Aspect of Philosophy*, Royce writes: "We confess at once that we want something much better than a postulate as the basis of our religion, in case we can get it. If postulates are to have any part in our religion, we want them to be justified by some ultimate religious certainty that is more than a postulate."[5] Indeed, his dissatisfaction with mere postulates dates at least back to 1883. Reflecting upon his philosophic career, Royce tells his 1915–16 Philosophy 9 course students:

> Lotze's way of getting out was a skeptical way. He asserted his postulates but regarded this as his own assertion. He qualified his statement of his own metaphysical views by saying "After all, my assertions about the ultimate nature of things are my view; I leave it to the verdict of God whom I do not presume to direct. *Gott weiss besser.*" That didn't give the kind of philosophy one wanted in order to direct men in their problems of life.[6]

Royce goes on to discuss how he came to his insight about the nature of error, leading to his "proof" for God's reality in *The Religious Aspect of Philosophy*. The insight into reality of error, along with a realization that postulates alone cannot get a person beyond the solipsism of the present moment, brought Royce to a stand against Lotze's "skeptical" way out of the Kantian dilemma of knowing the thing-in-itself. "This led me to a decided reversal of point of view which followed. My postulates may be mere attitudes toward the real. If that is the case, then error is at least possible. But what would be an error?"[7] Royce concludes instead with something I think is more than a Lotzean postulate: "The being of the world involves the interpretation of my problem."[8] He continues, "If there were no problem, if there were no interpretation, or if the interpretation were itself given, then the being of the world would be presented to an interpreting mind."[9] This may be a series of conditional statements, but for Royce it must be more than Lotzean "postulates." Despite Royce's comments about the inadequacy of postulates, Auxier's reading of Royce's philosophy is still a persuasive one because Royce's philosophic method is ultimately based on postulates, even if he does not quite say "*Gott weiss besser.*"

Ironically, the origin of Royce's hypothetical method of philosophizing is in the very work where he expresses his dissatisfaction with mere postulates, *The Religious Aspect of Philosophy*. In the ninth chapter of that work, he builds his philosophic method on a phenomenology of concept formation. In his phenomenology of concept formation, he describes the process of constituting objects of knowledge in Kantian terms, thus contending that objects in the external world are not given directly to us. Rather, objects (specifically objects of knowledge) are constructed out of our sense impressions. These sense impressions are then interpreted in accordance with our evolving conceptual and interpretative frameworks.

Additionally, a Roycean phenomenology considers "whatever external world there may be for us"[10] to be a postulate. This means that we do not know with any certainty that there is an external reality. Instead, any knowledge of the external world that we have is due to a "deliberate and courageous volition"[11] on our part. Indeed, our knowledge about external reality involves "a risk, for the sake of a higher end,"[12] with that higher end usually aiming to improve our ability to navigate around in an uncertain world and living better lives. It also allows us to predict the consequences of our actions with some probability, which further improves our ability to live in an often uncertain world.[13]

While he describes his phenomenology of concept formation only once, namely, in the ninth chapter of *The Religious Aspect of Philosophy*, it serves as the theoretical basis for all of his subsequent philosophical inquiries. This is so because Royce regards concepts and postulates to be the most basic and publicly accessible objects of knowledge (whether that knowledge is of a philosophical, religious, or scientific nature).[14] Such a phenomenology reminds us that philosophical knowledge, like all other human knowledge, is thoroughly constructed and only, at most, indirectly refers to the world we experience through our sense impressions and perceptions.[15] Our philosophical knowledge of reality is thoroughly constituted by concepts that we construct. As Royce writes: "all knowing is, in a very real sense, acting; it is, in fact, reacting and creation."[16] Since he never worked out an alternative philosophic method, I take this to be his method throughout his published works.

At this point one could object that my analysis of Royce's phenomenology of concept formation emphasizes what he calls the "outer form" of his argumentation, and that my emphasis neglects the "inner form" of his argumentation in *The Religious Aspect of Philosophy*, namely, his penetrating investigations into such concepts as right/wrong, good/evil, and error/truth. Yet, my reply to the above objection is twofold. First, I consider Royce's articulation and defense of his ethico-religious insight to be the inner form of *The Religious Aspect of Philosophy*. Second, and more importantly, one cannot simply ignore the outer form of his argumentation because it is his phenomenology of concept formation that complicates his attempt to demonstrate the necessary existence of God. Given Royce's understanding of philosophical knowledge in this text, how is it possible for us to construct a philosophical concept of something, for example, God, that we experience neither directly nor indirectly?

Since he cannot base his conception of God on anything that he actually experiences or could ever possibly experience, he reverts to Kantian transcendental argumentation. Indeed, we could interpret Royce's ontological argument as his answer to two epistemic questions: (1) What are the transcendental conditions for living an ethico-religious life? (2) What are the transcendental conditions for human knowledge acquisition? The way that Royce implements transcendental argumentation in *The Religious Aspect of Philosophy* makes his argument for God's existence an epistemic, or more accurately an onto-epistemic, one. Yet, this does not explain sufficiently how it is possible to construct a philosophical conception of something that we do not experience at all, nor does it explain how his philosophic method can adequately describe his ethico-religious insight, if it cannot adequately describe the central element of his insight: his conception of God.

The work where I think he comes closest to succeeding in this endeavor is in his 1895 lecture "The Conception of God," in whose first section he announces that his philosophical conception of God is only a philosophical conception. Yet he thinks that an adequate philosophical conception of God ought "to be able, in a measure, to translate into articulate terms the central mystery of our existence, and to get some notion about what is at the heart of the world."[17] Of course, he thinks that if any adequate philosophical proof for God's existence actually exists, then it would have to demonstrate how God's presence is at the heart of the world and is the related to the central mystery of our existence.[18] This means that our philosophical conception of God must correspond "to some living Reality"[19] in order for it to be a worthwhile one. Consequently, conceiving of God as a bare possibility is not a viable option for Royce. Nevertheless, he is willing to conceive of God initially in terms of a conceptual definition, then he demonstrates that his definition denotes an existent omniscient being; this conception serves as the central feature of his demonstration of God's existence[20]—a conclusion he believes to be valid because once we demonstrate that an omniscient being is indeed actual, the other traditional attributes associated with the divine in Western thought would necessarily follow.[21]

In addition, unlike everything else, an omniscient being is one in whom "all genuinely significant, all truly thinkable ideas would be seen as directly fulfilled, and fulfilled in his own experience."[22] This omniscient experience is accompanied by an immediate, intimate knowledge of all ideas and their relations to one another. For an omniscient being, then, its acts of experience and of cognition occur simultaneously.[23] Accordingly, an omniscient being is both absolute thought (i.e., a being who is cognizant of all actual and possible ideas and facts all at once) and absolute experience (i.e., a being who intimately and immediately experiences every actual and genuinely possible finite experiencer, including every actual and possible experience that experiencer might have).[24]

After introducing us to God *qua* philosophical concept, Royce lays all his cards on the table in the first paragraph of section two. There he explicitly states his central thesis: "that the very nature of human ignorance is such that you cannot conceive or define it apart from the assertion that there is, in truth, at the heart of the world, an Absolute and Universal Intelligence, for which thought and experience, so divided in us, are in complete and harmonious unity."[25] This makes it evident that Royce considers human ignorance to be the existential and ontological condition demonstrating that there is an omniscient being at the heart of our world. He views human ignorance in this way because it discloses the liminal character of our actual, fleeting, and fragmentary present experience. Accordingly, he thinks that our ignorance of anything beyond our immediately present experience motivates us to construct ideals that organize our present experience in relation to an overarching ideal realm of experience, at least seen as being ideal from our present experience.

This ideal experience would include all actual and possible experiences, facts, and states of affairs within itself. This ideal experience, in fact, is what we normally mean by *reality*,[26] and we acquire knowledge of reality only through the concepts we construct. For instance, scientific conceptions are examples of human concepts putting us in relation to this ideal experience.[27] Indeed, Royce makes the above point this way: "As a fact, direct human experience, apart from the elaborately devised indirect contrivances of conceptual thought, knows nothing of [reality]."[28] In the case of our natural environing world, we acquire knowledge of it to the extent that our scientific hypotheses are verifiable in terms of our future experiences, specifically the ones that resemble the past experiences under which those hypotheses were first constructed.[29]

However, unlike our scientific knowledge of the natural, environing world, our philosophical knowledge of God is not verifiable in any actual human experience, but is presupposed to be the basis of all actual and possible human experience. Using classical logic, he argues that "every possible proposition involves a categorical proposition. Every *if* implies an *is*."[30] We can interpret this statement to mean that every hypothetical proposition presupposes some actual, concrete experiencer who asserts that proposition. Like the full-blooded idealist that he sometimes is, Royce takes the above point a step further and declares his adherence to panexperientialism: "All knowledge is of something experienced. For this means that nothing actually exists save what is somewhere experienced."[31] This is why he does not think that there is any *bare* possibility, or possibilities existing apart from some actual being that experiences them.[32] It follows from his panexperientialism that God is the absolute actuality that serves as the ground for all genuinely possible experiences, and thus knows "all that is or that genuinely can be known."[33] Otherwise we would be trapped, Royce thinks, within a solipsism of the present moment, from which we would be unable to acquire knowledge about anything, including ourselves.

Moreover, God is the one who enables us to live in a meaningful world, and not simply a world of disjointed facts. This makes God the conceptual expression of our ethico-religious postulate. Royce describes the ontological import of his ethico-religious postulate and how our experience of ignorance provides us with the existential evidence to construct an adequate conception of God:

> [F]or such an experience, this constitution of the finite is a fact determined from an absolute point of view, and every finite incompleteness and struggle appears as a part of a whole in whose wholeness the fragments find their true place, the ideas their realization, the seeking its fulfillment, and our whole life its truth, and so its eternal rest,—that peace which transcends the storms of its agony and its restlessness. For this agony and restlessness

are the very embodiment of an incomplete experience, of a finite ignorance.

Do you ask, then: What in our human world does God get revealed?—what manifests his glory? I answer: Our ignorance, our fallibility, our imperfection, and so, as forms of this ignorance and imperfection, our experience of longing, of strife, of pain, of error,—yes, of whatever, as finite, declares that its truth lies in its limitation, and so lies beyond itself. These things, wherein we taste the bitterness of our finitude, are what they are because they mean more than they contain, imply what is beyond them, refuse to exist by themselves, and, at the very moment of confessing their own fragmentary falsity, assure us of the reality of that fulfillment which is the life of God.[34]

Viewed in terms of his phenomenology of concept formation, God could be interpreted as the concept we construct to eliminate the fragmentariness and incompleteness of every actual experience and affirm the unitary nature of reality. Hence, the philosophical conception of God is not merely an object of knowledge, as all other concepts are, but is *the* object that corresponds to the feature of reality that is eternal. God, then, is a philosophic postulate, plain and simple.

Whether he called it the Absolute, All-Knower, God, or the Interpreter Spirit of the Universal Community of Interpretation,[35] Royce considers the absolute to be eternal—not in the sense of being timeless but in the sense of being all time-inclusive.[36] For that reason Royce conceives of God as the one who experiences all past, present, and future moments simultaneously, but these temporal moments occur within a genuine temporal succession.[37] He also conceives of God as the one who experiences us and our specific life plans as "identically a part of God's experience, i.e., not similar to a portion of God's experience, but identically the same as such portion; and . . . identically part of God's own attentively selected and universal plan."[38]

Nevertheless, one could object that the above characterization of Royce's conception of God is only applicable to what Oppenheim has classified as the early Royce (that is, the Royce of 1883–95).[39] One could grant the contention that the early Royce's God is a philosophical postulate; however, one could still object that the God of Royce's middle years (1896–1911) is less like a theoretical construct and more like a living, dynamic individual who suffers alongside us.[40] The God of Royce's late years (1912–16) appears to be even less a theoretical construction than his early conceptions of God, since it is based on a plausible interpretation of actual early twentieth-century Christian experience.[41] By 1912, through an intensive study of Peircean semiotics and modern symbolic logic, he conceives of God as the processive Interpreter Spirit of the Community of Interpretation.[42] This processive God seems to be radically different from both the onto-epistemic God of *The Religious Aspect of Philosophy* and the modal and existential God of "The Conception of God" address.

Nevertheless, to say that Royce's late conception of God is based upon a plausible interpretation of Christian religious experience does not make it any less couched in the language of hypothetical postulates than his earliest conception of God in *The Religious Aspect of Philosophy*. Here is an example of the late Royce describing God in hypothetical terms:

> We have no ground whatever for believing that there is any real world except the ground furnished by our experience, and by the fact that, in addition to our perceptions and our conceptions, we have problems upon our hands which need interpretation. Our fundamental postulate is: *The world is the interpretation of the problem which it presents.* . . .
>
> Our Doctrine of Signs extends to the whole world the same fundamental principle. The World is the Community. The world contains its own interpreter. Its processes are infinite in their temporal varieties. But their interpreter, the spirit of this universal community,—compares and, through a real life, interprets them all.[43]

This means that even in *The Problem of Christianity* we are still left with a philosophical conception of God that is articulated in hypothetical and conceptual terms. And this is problematic, given that our philosophic conception of God cannot denote something actually existing due to the fact that (a) we can construct philosophic concepts only out of what we can experience and (b) we cannot experience God directly for Royce.

What is left of Royce's ethico-religious insight if it cannot transcend its problematic status as a hypothetical postulate? What I prefer to do is read Royce as though his philosophic propositions, especially his conception of God, describe actual features of our world. My interpretation of Royce's thought aims to describe how Royce's ethico-religious insight could be described philosophically if one bracketed the problematic nature of his philosophic method.

I realize that this approach does not solve the problematic nature of Royce's philosophic method. What it does accomplish, though, is a reexamination of Royce's philosophy in light of his ethico-religious insight. And that is sufficient for our purposes. What I would like to do for the remainder of this book is compare Royce's ethico-religious insight with two other twentieth-century philosophers who based their philosophies on an ethico-religious insight: Martin Luther King, Jr. and Emmanuel Levinas.

SIX

KING'S BELOVED COMMUNITY, ROYCE'S METAPHYSICS

The philosophy of Martin Luther King, Jr., can be characterized as a confluence of several amiable theological and philosophical perspectives. Charles R. Johnson, for example, characterizes it as being a "complex yet ethically coherent philosophy"—a mixture of Walter Rauschenbusch's social gospel, Boston personalism, and Mohandas Gandhi's love-ethic and method of nonviolence.[1] While these ideas are important to King's philosophy, he was unquestionably most influenced by the African American Baptist tradition.[2] He accepted Boston personalism, the social gospel movement, and Gandhi's love ethic and nonviolence to the extent that they strengthened two important convictions he acquired from his Baptist background:

An earlier version of this chapter was presented at the Joint Group session of the Society for the Philosophy of Creativity, the Personalist Group, and the Society for the Study of Process Philosophy during the 2005 American Philosophical Association Central Division Meeting, Chicago, Illinois, on April 29, 2005. I especially thank Rufus Burrow, Jr., and Stephen Bickham for their insightful comments on my earlier presentation.

(1) that there is a personal God and (2) that all human persons are worthy of being treated with respect and dignity because they are created in God's image.[3] This is not the occasion to examine in depth the influence that Boston personalism, Gandhi's thought, Rauschenbusch's social gospel, or the African American Baptist tradition had on King's philosophy. (Even though an in depth examination of the influence that African American Christian tradition had on King's philosophy would be a welcomed additional to King scholarship, especially one that delves into the thought of Benjamin E. Mays, George Kelsey, A. D. Williams, and Howard Thurman.) Instead, this chapter examines the similarities between King's and Royce's personalisms through their notions of *agape* and the Beloved Community. It also examines how Royce's personalism[4] could lessen a notable conceptual weakness in King's Beloved Community and how King's personalism does the same for Royce's philosophy.

Martin Luther King, Jr.'s Personalism: Agape *and the Beloved Community*

Separating King's notions of *agape* and the Beloved Community from his overall philosophic thought is virtually impossible. I will describe the roles these concepts play in the two major periods of King's public philosophy.[5] The first period starts in December 1955, when he became the lead organizer of the Montgomery bus boycott, and ends with the enactment of the Voting Rights Bill in August 1965; the second period goes from the fall of 1965 to his assassination on April 4, 1968.[6]

The most central theses in King's philosophy were born during the first of these periods. Among these theses is King's doctrine of nonviolence. Johnson describes King's doctrine this way: "nonviolence—in words and actions—must be understood not merely as a strategy for protest, but as a Way, a daily praxis people must strive to translate into each and every one of their deeds."[7] We should remember that King committed himself personally to nonviolence only after he recognized the efficacy of *agape* in real-world situations, and not until after he had meditated and prayed about what he should do after his house was bombed on January 30, 1956.[8] Until then he had agreed with Reinhold Niebuhr that aggressive nonviolent protest was the only practical means for blacks to demand from whites, especially in the South, recognition for being fellow Americans and, more importantly, as fellow human persons, endowed by their Creator with the same inalienable rights to life, liberty, and the pursuit of happiness.[9] We also should not forget that even after the Montgomery bus boycott began, he initially "had armed guards around his house and even applied for a permit to carry a gun in his car,"[10] and even after his conversion to nonviolence in his own life, he recognized that violence was still acceptable for protecting one's family or home.[11] Yet, he did not count such uses of violence as something we should do ideally and they definitely do not contribute to the actualization of the Beloved Community.[12]

King realized that nonviolence is not only an effective practical means of a group of oppressed persons to demand that their oppressors cease dehumanizing and depersonalizing them and respect their God-given freedom as persons, it is also the most moral means of transforming the lives of both groups for the better. Violence, on the other hand, not only brutalizes the oppressed physically, mentally, and spiritually, but also dehumanizes the oppressors. Nonviolence, then, is a form of what I would call psycho-spiritual therapy for both the oppressed and the oppressor if the former is willing to endure suffering without lashing out, and creatively transform their suffering into positive moral energy. This positive moral energy has the potential to transform the oppressor into a fellow sibling in the Beloved Community, or at least force the oppressor to respect the personhood and somebodiness of those they have oppressed.[13] He describes the results of this psycho-spiritual therapy in *Why We Can't Wait*, where he discusses the status of the civil rights movement in 1963:

> Nonviolence had tremendous psychological importance to the Negro. He had to win and to vindicate his dignity in order to merit and enjoy his self-esteem. He had to let white men know that the picture of him as a clown—irresponsible, resigned and

believing in his own inferiority—was a stereotype with no validity. This method was grasped by the Negro masses because it embodied the dignity of struggle, of moral conviction and self-sacrifice. The Negro was able to face his adversary, to concede him a physical advantage and to defeat him because the superior force of the oppressor had become powerless.

To measure what this meant to the Negro may not be easy. But I am convinced that the courage and discipline with which Negro thousands accepted nonviolence healed the internal wounds of Negro millions who did not themselves march in the streets or sit in the jails of the South. One need not participate directly in order to be involved. For Negroes all over this nation, to identify with the movement, to have pride in those who were the principals, and to give moral, financial or spiritual support were to restore to them some of the pride and honor which had been stripped from them over the centuries.[14]

Nonviolence, when practiced well and sincerely, enables its practitioners to act in *agapic* love toward other persons, even those persons who have historically oppressed them. Indeed, King's adherence to nonviolence led him to adopt a second related thesis: we should practice *agape* in our daily lives and have our nonviolent conduct be an extension of our *agapic* love toward other persons. On a human level, since this is the only level of reality that we have any chance of describing competently, *agape* is "the ability to unconditionally love something not for what it currently is (for at a particular moment it might be quite unlovable, like segregationist George Wallace in the early 1960s) but instead for what it could become, a teleological love that recognizes everything as process, not product, and sees beneath the surface to a thing's potential for positive change."[15] Anyone familiar with the personalistic ethics advanced in Brightman's *Moral Laws*[16] and Walter G. Muelder's *Moral Law in Christian Social Ethics*[17] should recognize the connection King makes between *agape* and what Brightman calls the "Law of the Ideal of Personality"[18] and what Muelder calls "The Law of the Ideal of Community."[19] Living according to *agape* obligates persons to live such a life where they "take up the materials of their lives and create the plan of a harmonious whole that they aim to realize."[20] But *agape* is not merely a regulative ideal for us to live by; it is also a part of our concrete reality. Indeed, in a way it is as concrete as any one of us, if not more so. Moreover, it operates as the spiritual "force" enabling those of us willing to live by it to create communities of goodwill and mutual respect with other persons where there were once none.[21] Yet, King's notion of *agape* is more than something he borrows from Brightman's and Muelder's personalistic ethics. It is the result of his creative synthesis of several thinkers' conception of love, including Paul Tillich, George Davis, L. Harold DeWolf, Howard Thurman, Paul Ramsey, and Anders Nygren.[22]

What does *agape* mean for King? First and foremost, *agape* "is not a sentimental or affectionate emotion,"[23] rather it "means understanding, redeeming good will for all men. It is an overflowing love which is purely spontaneous, unmotivated, groundless, and creative."[24] At times, *agape* might require us to perform acts that are contrary to our immediate self-interests since it is unconditionally and universally altruistic. But it is not a vacuous love for an abstraction, for example, "humanity." It obligates us to respond to the actual physical, psychological, and spiritual needs of our fellow persons—whether they are our neighbors, our colleagues, our acquaintances, our fellow citizens, or citizens of another political state.[25]

Once King's recognition of *agape* led him to regard all life as interrelated, he could not help but recognize that whatever we do affects other persons directly or indirectly, often in unforeseen and detrimental ways. His affirmation of this truth leads him to the third central thesis of his philosophy: the interrelatedness and interdependence of everything in the world. King expresses this thesis when he contends in his "Letter from Birmingham Jail":

> I am cognizant of the interrelatedness of all communities and states. I cannot sit idly by in Atlanta and not be concerned about what happens in Birmingham. Injustice anywhere is a threat to justice everywhere. We are all caught in an inescapable network of mutuality, tied in a single garment of destiny. Whatever affects one directly, affects all indirectly.[26]

This recognition of the interrelatedness of all human persons naturally moves us directly to King's notion of the Beloved Community.

King's Beloved Community seems simple enough to describe. It is the community that we create whenever we dwell with other persons in the spirit of *agapic* love. Insofar as we recognize the personhood of our fellow human persons—regardless of the level of their cognitive functioning, socioeconomic status, gender, ethnicity, race, religious affiliation, political affiliation, sexual orientation, and so forth—and they do likewise, then we are actualizing the Beloved Community on earth. Recognizing their personhood does not mean that we assimilate them into a certain way of life. It means that we accept them for who they are, but expect them to do likewise—all without using physical or psychological violence in our efforts to create a Beloved Community.[27]

There is a problem with King's notion of the Beloved Community, however. Sometimes, he speaks of it as an operative and partially actualizable ideal. According to this interpretation, it is at best an operative and regulative ideal that has some efficacy in our daily lives to the extent that we view it as a norm of our interpersonal relations. Other times, King speaks of it as something that could possibly be actualized fully someday.[28] This apparent tension in King's understanding of the idea might be because of his acceptance of a sort of eschatology prevalent in the African American Baptist tradition[29] and having a Hegelian-inspired *Zeitgeist* grafted onto it. Let me quote James Cone's assessment of the influence that King's eschatology had on his view of the Beloved Community:

> [By 1964] King believed that because God was involved in the freedom struggles, they could not be halted. Victory was inevitable. Successes in the civil rights and Third World liberation movements and King's own deep faith in God's loving justice combined to give him an optimistic hope that freedom was not too far away.[30]
>
> It was Martin's hope which sustained him in the midst of controversy, enabling him to make a solidarity with the victims of the world, even though he failed to achieve the justice for which he

gave his life. Martin's hope was derived from his religious faith, and it enabled him to see the certainty of victory in the context of an apparent defeat.[31]

Some King scholars, for example, Ansbro, have done considerable work to resolve this apparent tension in King's philosophy by arguing that King's Beloved Community is a realistic, regulative ideal.[32] However, there is at least another legitimate way of interpreting King's concept that rejects Ansbro's interpretation, taken up by one of the most recognized institutional organs of King's legacy, the King Center. The Beloved Community is "not a lofty utopian goal to be confused with the rapturous image of the Peaceable Kingdom, in which lions and lambs coexist in idyllic harmony. Rather, The Beloved Community was for him a realistic, achievable goal that could be attained by a critical mass of people committed to and trained in the philosophy and methods of nonviolence."[33] The King Center then lists several concrete goals that the Beloved Community could actualize, given the proper economic, political, and communal resources. These goals include empowering the poor economically; feeding the hungry locally and worldwide; building shelter for the homeless; getting local, regional, national and international governmental organizations to provide adequate health care for those who do not have access to it; and combating racial, ethnic, and all other forms of discrimination that prevent us from further actualizing the Beloved Community, both locally and globally.[34]

Judith Green's recent writing on King's Beloved Community further displays its unresolved tension.[35] Sometimes, she writes about it as an actual community,[36] with leaders and actual "volunteer members."[37] Other times, she writes about it as an operative ideal acted upon by actual persons in an effort to actualize more and more of the Beloved Community in their lives, locally, nationally, and internationally.[38]

This apparent tension in King's notion of the Beloved Community becomes more pronounced during the second period of his public career, when, in the fall of 1965, he "envisioned himself not merely as a Southern civil rights leader, but instead as a man obligated to promote his belief in the 'beloved community' and peace on the world stage—a stance that would make him the first international celebrity to oppose the Vietnam War."[39] By 1968 he had done some work on developing a systematic criticism of the United States for its imperialism abroad and its unjust discrimination against racial minorities and the economically disadvantaged at home. But his unyielding faith in the inevitability of the Beloved Community's actualization probably exacerbated his disillusionment with most of white America and its unwillingness to actualize the Beloved Community by supporting anti-poverty policies, international movements against colonization and oppression, efforts to end American imperialist policies abroad (particularly in Vietnam), anti-discrimination policies, and policies that empower non-Caucasian minorities with genuine political and economic power, instead of supporting an impotent tokenism.[40] Yet, his eschatology—which affirms that despite whatever happens today, God's moral order shall prevail in the end—guided his steps and energized him to take unpopular stances on the behalf of the ideal of the Beloved Community.[41] King gave the best articulation of his eschatology concerning the Beloved Community a day prior to his death.[42]

Nevertheless, he also preached a sermon at the National Episcopal Cathedral on the Sunday before his death, where he stated that we should not sit idly by and wait for the divine to actualize the Beloved Community.[43] In that sermon he preached that we are the only ones who can actualize the Beloved Community or that it will not be actualized at all.[44] King's philosophy ends with the unresolved creative tension between an eschatology guaranteeing God's moral victory and his personalist stance contending that we are co-creators of the Beloved Community, with God being the anchor of all our efforts.

Royce's Personalistic Notions of Agape and the Beloved Community

Now that we have described King's notions of *agape* and the Beloved Community, let us turn our attention to Josiah Royce's thoughts on *agape* and the beloved community. We should remember that Royce coined the phase "the beloved community."[45] When Royce mentions the Beloved Community in *The Problem of Christianity*, he does so in his selective genetic description of Christianity in the first volume. He does not give the philosophical dimension of that notion until the second volume, and then he uses such phrases as "Community of Interpretation" and "Universal Community" to refer to the Beloved Community. Something similar is true for Royce's discussion of *agape*. Gary Herstein rightly notes in his text on the Roycean origins of the Beloved Community: "Royce never explicitly uses the term [*agape*] in *The Problem of Christianity*. [Anders] Nygren's treatment of the subject, and the recovery of the term for Christian thought, didn't appear until almost two decades after Royce's lectures were published. This does not mean that the concept is absent from Royce's thought. On the contrary, Royce's thoughts about Christian love pervade the text."[46]

Where I disagree with Herstein is with what he identifies as the term that Royce uses as the equivalent of *agape* in *The Problem of Christianity*. It is not *loyalty* that functions like *agape* in *The Problem of Christianity*, as Herstein argues; it is the will to interpret. Herstein does have a valid point, though, when he identifies that *loyalty* functions like *agape* in Royce's writings, particularly in Royce's *The Philosophy of Loyalty*. However, Royce's notion of loyalty, even his spiritualized understanding expressed in the phrase "loyalty to loyalty," falls short of *agape* because it does not adequately describe the transformative nature of living according to *agapic* love. I think that Royce's "will to interpret," in its most spiritual sense, does adequately describe this phenomenon. With that said, let me describe Royce's notion of *agape* and the Beloved Community by describing how the will to interpret and the community of interpretation fits into his ethico-religious metaphysics. The explication below is heavily dependent on my analysis of *The Problem of Christianity* in Chapter 3.

The will to interpret, endowed to us by the divine Interpreter Spirit, enables us to build communities with others where there were once none. It also serves as the means for us to establish communities of memory, where persons agree to interpret certain past events in a similar way, and communities of hope, where persons share similar goals, anticipations, and expectations for the future.[47] No community, for Royce, is a genuine one without possessing both of these characteristics; it must both be a community of memory and a community of hope. Without a shared memory and shared goals, anticipation, and expectations of the future, all we have is an aggregate of persons in the same geographical location.[48] However, the will to interpret is more than the animating force behind us establishing local communities of persons; when recognized as the spirit of the Beloved Community immanent in the world, it is what unites us in community with the divine.

Spiritually speaking, then, interpretation is the will to interpret, which in Christianity is symbolized by the acts of the Holy Spirit, unifying Christians together to form actual churches and thus joining them together to be members of the invisible yet partially actual and influential church. Royce calls this church the Beloved Community. We can only partially actualize the Beloved Community in our acts in the spatio-temporal world. It remains, for the most part, an ideal. Many philosophers unjustly discriminate against it due to their prejudice for the fully actual over the partially actual and partially ideal. I admit that other philosophers are rightly worried that such an ideal might manifest itself in detrimental ways, such as totalitarian regimes that confuse their human-constructed ideals for the ideal of the Beloved Community and oppress their fellow persons in its name. But there is always a danger that any ideal, however good, can be perverted.

Here is another way to describe Royce's thoughts on *agape* and the Beloved Community. The will to interpret (which in its most spiritual manifestation is *agapic love*) is a radical openness to certain possibilities that become imaginable to human persons when they touch the everlasting divine and recognize their dependence on others for their own well-being. This act of recognition motivates them to pursue a life of loyalty to the ideal of the Beloved Community. From their perspective, the Beloved Community becomes as a genuine reality to them, and their entire way of being in the world changes so that their ethico-religious awareness becomes their primary way of interpreting themselves and their environing world. Such a shift in our way of being would have us be emotionally, intellectually, and spiritually empathetic with our fellows, for we live in an interrelated community of persons who depend on one another to live well-lived lives, or at least good lives, in which we are free to pursue our individual life-plans. This would include helping others live out their life-plans and lessening the detrimental conflicts between persons.[49]

Strengthening the Conceptual Weaknesses in King's and Royce's Notions of the Beloved Community

We have noted the creative tension in King's notion of the Beloved Community. This ambiguity in the very nature of King's Beloved Community might be more rhetorically effective than a conceptually consistent description of it, given that anyone listening to him or reading him has at least two possible ways of interpreting it. Nevertheless, there is a way for King to ease this tension without sacrificing any of his rhetoric power (I hope) and adding conceptual consistency to his philosophy: one could interpret King's Beloved Community in Roycean terms.

Indeed, a Roycean metaphysics of community enables King to say that we are able to actualize the Beloved Community, however partially we may do so; that the divine desires us to actualize that ideal community; and that it is likely that we would actualize more and more of it once more and more persons truly live their lives by that ideal. Instead of juggling between personalistic language, where the Beloved Community is more ideal than actual, and more traditional Christian language, where the Beloved Community is an inevitability, King could say that the Beloved Community becomes actual "only when [we] are *actually* working alongside, responding to, building trust with, and becoming trustworthy with concrete others in their more local communities."[50] In this sense I agree with Ansbro's attempt to define King's Beloved Community as an ideal that we can partially, but never completely, actualize in human history.

A Roycean metaphysics of community also fits King's philosophy because, like King, "Royce stresses the need for local communities to develop a sense of pride in their origins and accomplishments"[51] and "encourages communities to build and create distinctive character."[52] They both also think that these communities should seek out one another and create larger communities where certain values and ideals—for example, the dignity of human life and respect for one's own and other persons' bodily integrity—connect them together. I grant that expecting actual communities to actualize such values and ideals completely is pie-in-the-sky utopianism, but expecting them to actualize these values and ideals to the best of their abilities is realistic. I, like King and Royce, would say that pursuing such ideals to our utmost ability is realistic because given the unprecedented interrelatedness of human persons worldwide not doing so could mean us being the victims of material impoverishment, physical violence, and/or psychological harm or mean us inflicting material impoverishment, physical violence, and/or psychological harm on others.

But King's philosophy is not the only one where there is a conceptual weakness in its notion of the Beloved Community. There is something that King's philosophy can do to ease what I regard as an outright contradiction in Royce's later philosophy: His attempt to hold onto his ideal of the Beloved Community while unequivocally advocating war against the Central Powers (Germany in particular) in World War I as a legitimate means of advancing the Beloved Community.[53] However justified or unjustified Royce's anger, bitterness, and resentment at Germany might have been during the last years of his life, his partisan pro-war stance does not square with his professed hope in the Beloved Community. Here is an abbreviated argument showing how Royce's pro-war stance is at the very least contrary to his own ideal of the Beloved Community:

1. The Beloved Community is built only by *agapic* acts.
2. *Agape* is, by its very nature, nonviolent.
3. Royce advocates the acceptability of measured violence to maintain the possibility for us to build a Beloved Community.

4. He further thinks that such violence, because it maintains the possibility for us to build a Beloved Community, contributes to the ideal of the Beloved Community.
5. Hence, certain acts of violence are acceptable means to contribute to the actualization of the Beloved Community.
6. But violent acts cannot actualize the ideal of the Beloved Community because they would betray the very ideal that they aim to actualize. At best, someone other than the one who committed those violent acts could creatively transform the consequences of those violent acts into circumstances where more and more persons would have better opportunities to actualize the Beloved Community in their everyday lives than they were before those violent acts occurred.
7. Therefore, Royce's acceptance of violence as a means to actualize the ideal of the Beloved Community is at the very least contrary to the spirit of that ideal.

Royce would not have had his political stance on World War I contradict his own ideal of the Beloved Community if he could have realized that violent means can never create *agapic* ends. To paraphrase King, only *agapic* means actualize genuinely *agapic* ends. King's advice to us in 1966 applies equally well to the Royce of 1915: "[V]iolence, even in self-defense, creates more problems than it solves. Only a refusal to hate or kill can put an end to the chain of violence in the world and lead us toward a community where man can live together without fear."[54] I only wish that Royce had drawn strength from the conceptual and spiritual resources present in his own philosophy to prevent himself from straying away from its deepest-held philosophical (and religious) convictions.

Concluding Remarks

I would like to end this chapter with a few comments about the lessons that King's and Royce's ethico-religious thought could teach us today. I would like to do this despite the weaknesses in both King's and Royce's ethico-religious thought, and the sometimes implausible and impossible demands that they make on us. Both King and Royce teach us that idealism—not a weird Berkeleyan idealism, but a personalistic ethical idealism—is a concrete and (dare I say it) a realistic philosophy because it realizes that we first have to change our interpretation of human existence before we can live better, more ethical lives. They think that viewing ourselves as part of an interconnected and personal world would lead us to live such lives that we would recognize that if any one of us suffers or is oppressed, then we all suffer and are oppressed. Therefore, we should do everything within our financial and personal power to equip oppressed persons with the means to live enriching lives and establish communities where they are not oppressed and depersonalized. But none of this can be effectively done until we first get a glimpse of the ideal of the Beloved Community and change the way we think and act to conform to it. King and Royce did not expect anyone to live up to the ideal of the Beloved Community. Nor do I expect any one of us to do so now. The main lesson that King and Royce teach us is this: If we try our best to live up to the ideal of the Beloved Community, and we inspire other persons to do so, then we would amaze ourselves with how much we could change the world, or at least our little corner of it.

SEVEN

COUPLING ROYCE'S TEMPORALISM WITH LEVINASIAN INSIGHTS

In this chapter I will address a serious problem with Royce's ethics and how that problem causes his ethics to be an inadequate mode of expressing his ethico-religious insight. The serious problem with Royce's ethics is that it neglects the origins of ethical experience. Instead, he conceives of ethics as the rational inquiry into how we ought to live. One cannot fault Royce for conceiving ethics in this manner,

---

Earlier versions of this chapter were presented over a thirteen-month period. An earlier version of the first section of this chapter was presented at the 29th Annual Midsouth Philosophy Conference, held at the University of Memphis in Memphis, Tennessee, on February 19, 2005. I thank Jason Bell for his constructive criticism when he commented on that presentation. I also thank the conference attendees who stayed until the last session of that conference to listen to my presentation. A much shorter version of this chapter was presented at the 33rd Annual Society for the Advancement of American Philosophy conference, held in San Antonio, Texas, on March 10, 2006. I thank Anthony Steinbock for reading that presentation in advance and offering helpful suggestions about how to improve it. I also thank Kim Garchar for her constructive criticism and insightful comments when she commented on that presentation. This chapter would not have existed in its present form without their assistance.

given that this conception of ethics is the most prevalent one in the Western philosophic tradition.

There is a danger with this conception of ethics, though; if often seems to consider a person as having moral worth only to the extent that we rationally recognize them as persons. Hopefully, the reason why such a state of affairs is a dangerous one will become more evident later in this chapter.

What I will do in this chapter is critique Royce's ethics from the standpoint of Emmanuel Levinas's phenomenology, as articulated in *Totality and Infinity* (1961)[1] and *Otherwise than Being, Or Beyond Essence* (1974).[2] I have chosen to critique Royce's ethics from a Levinasian standpoint because both Royce and Levinas place an ethico-religious insight at the heart of their philosophies. They both also agree that all human experience is essentially temporal.[3] These similarities should make it easier for a Roycean "ethical temporalism"[4] to integrate some Levinasian insights into its own description of human temporality, thus lessening the dangerousness of Royce's ethics.

Royce's Temporalism: Viewing Its Theoretical Structure and Ethical Import

Given that most contemporary philosophers do not consider Royce to be a temporalist philosopher, I am obliged to provide the reader with a relatively concise description of Royce's temporalism, which I will base on a synthesis of "The Temporal and the Eternal"[5] chapter of *The World and the Individual* and his 1910 essay "The Reality of the Temporal."[6] Following Charles Sherover in *The Human Experience of Time*,[7] I shall concentrate almost exclusively on Royce's description of human temporality. Then, in order to emphasize the ethical import of Royce's temporalism, I will place my account of his temporalism within his philosophy's larger ethico-religious framework.

In "The Temporal and the Eternal" Royce performs a proto-phenomenology of internal time-consciousness. I say "proto-phenomenology" rather than "phenomenology," especially in the Husserlian sense, because Royce's phenomenological descriptions are not concerned with unveiling the eidetic structures of phenomena; they, instead, serve as the descriptive basis of his ontology. In his proto-phenomenology of internal time-consciousness, he describes how the temporal modalities of past, present and future are actually abstractions from our immediate awareness of the significant events in our lives.[8] That is, we first experience memorable events as having a specific duration, marked by a relatively determinate beginning and a relatively determinate end. Then, from these events, we interpret the world as being one where some events are irrevocably past, others are presently occurring, and still others having yet to occur. Consequently, we experience the world temporally, not because we directly intuit the temporal structure of the world as it is in-itself, but because we are temporal creatures who cannot experience it in any other way.

As a result of his proto-phenomenological investigation of our internal time-consciousness, Royce contends that our perceptual time,[9] or "specious present," is our initial mode of temporal awareness. When we experience the world perceptually, we select only a few of the innumerable events that we presently experience as being meaningful ones, thereby becoming the foci of our selective attention. The duration, or time-span, of our selective attention lasts maybe a few seconds or so and is, according to Royce, the "more strictly temporal sense" of the present.[10]

There is another sense of the present other than the "specious present." This second present is the conceptual present,[11] or the present seen as a time span that becomes determinate only after we decide what smaller time spans should be considered part of it. The conceptual present could be merely a few seconds long, like our specious present, or extend over many millennia. The flexibility of the conceptual present allows us to group many otherwise distinct time spans together and regard them as moments in a larger one to suit our specific purposes.[12]

When we examine our internal time-consciousness further, we observe that while we live immediately *in* the present moment, our temporal awareness seems to extend beyond our immediate perceptions of the world. This leads us to assert that the past and the future are, like the present, ontologically real modalities of temporality. In fact, the past is real precisely because it is actual. And the past is actual because the present could not be what it is without the past carrying itself forward into the present. On the other hand, the future is real even though it is indeterminate and non-actual. For many contemporary metaphysicians, the future could only be considered real if and only if it is actual somehow, for example, as a not-yet-accessed part of space-time as it is in the spotlight theory of time. According to them, a non-actual future cannot be real. Nonetheless, Royce would probably reply that the future's non-actuality should not prevent it from being considered real, if we define *real* in terms of something's efficacy in the world, specifically in our lives. In this sense of the term *real*, the future is indeed real.

Another result of Royce's investigation of our internal time-consciousness is that he views "will," or purposive creative force,[13] as what unifies our past, our perceptual present, our conceptual present, and our future into a larger temporal unity. As Royce writes in the third section of "The Temporal and the Eternal":

> To my mind . . . time, as the form of the will, is (in so far as we can undertake to define at all the detailed structure of finite reality) to be viewed as the most pervasive form of all finite experience, whether human or extra-human. In pursuing its goals, the Self [i.e., person] lives in time. And, to our view, every real being in the universe, in so far as it has not won union with the ideal, is pursuing that ideal; and, accordingly, so far as we can see, is living in time.[14]

Given the above description of human (and extra-human) temporality, we could describe how Royce views the temporal structure of human persons along these lines. The temporal structure of human persons consists of three interrelated selves—a past, present, and future self. Our past self consists of all the events that each of us has undergone and brought about up to the present moment. This self is our definite self because we cannot undo anything we have done or undergone prior to the present moment. We can only reinterpret our past through our present circumstances and future expectations, anticipations, and commitments. Our present self is our immediate perceptual awareness of the world and the vague experiential moment where our past self intermingles with our future self. In *The Problem of Christianity*, Royce speaks of this self as the one who "interprets" the past self to the future self.[15] Such an act of interpretation is an act of will par excellence. Our future self, in turn, is us in our potentiality; that is, it is us in our relative indeterminacy.

It seems that the above approach to temporality leads Royce to say that the temporal world, as experienced by human persons, is "a sequence of novel and individual events, each expressing somebody's present will to do something unique, and to find his [sic] own place in the world" in "The Reality of the Temporal."[16] As we have noted above, Royce thinks that the temporality of human existence is ultimately an expression of our (creative) will. Furthermore, the world time-order is seen as an all-inclusive temporal field—or, more appropriately, an all-inclusive temporal horizon—where all finite beings pursue whatever potentialities they intend to pursue within their specific time-spans, with each and every finite life-span participating in the eternal time-span that is God. We have to remember, though, that eternal, for Royce, does not mean timeless, "but the totality of temporal events viewed precisely as a totality."[17] In other words, Royce's eternal is everlasting, not timeless. Consequently, his understanding of the "eternal" is very similar to Brightman's "eternal" in "A Temporalist View of God."[18]

On this point, Royce writes: "The temporal not merely implies the eternal; in its wholeness it constitutes the eternal,—namely, the total decision of the world will, wherein the loyal will to be rational [which presupposes the loyal will to be ethical] finds its own fulfillment."[19]

However, we should remember that Royce writes in such works as *The Philosophy of Loyalty* and *The Problem of Christianity* that we can only partially actualize them in our daily encounters and interactions with other human persons.

What we have here is the structural scaffolding of Royce's temporalism. Nevertheless, I do not think that Royce would have us end our explication of his temporalism this way. He would probably caution us that this formal structure is intelligible only when it is situated in his idealistic, ethico-religious metaphysics.[20]

Respecting Royce's wishes on this matter, here is an account of his temporalism that situates it within his larger ethico-religious metaphysics: We human persons are not substantive entities, but ethical selves.[21] Being ethical selves means that we are neither empirical egos[22] nor Aristotelian *ousia*,[23] definable only by our empirically observable characteristics. We are primarily, and primordially, temporal creatures who maintain our identity through the life-plan we live out. By choosing a life-plan that motivates us to develop our fullest potential most effectively, we fulfill a task that only we as unique finite persons could fulfill—namely, to advance the spiritual union of all persons by our recognizing the individuality and uniqueness of all persons and by our being mindful of our dependence on one another and on the divine Spirit for our very existence.[24]

Levinas's Ethical Phenomenology: Encountering the Other as the Origin of Our Temporality

Let us end our explication of Royce's temporalism for a while and describe Levinas's phenomenology of human temporality. Levinas thinks that human temporality originates in our encounters with the Other (*l'Autre*) *qua* other human person (*l'autrui*). These moments of encountering the Other are ones where the non-phenomenal reveals itself at the threshold of our phenomenal experience—at least this is the case if we restrict phenomenality to the realm of cognitive and perceptual representation, or, as Levinas calls it in *Totality and Infinity*, "disclosure."[25]

As a phenomenology of the non-phenomenal, a Levinasian phenomenology has to transcend the limitations of Husserl's phenomenological and transcendental reductions[26] in order to investigate how the alterity of the Other acquires its meaning for us in our non-phenomenal encounter with the Other *qua* other person. To transcend Husserl's phenomenology, and its impotence in describing the non-phenomenal as non-phenomenal, a Levinasian phenomenology has to center around an *epoché* that not only puts the ontological status of one's encounter with other persons in abeyance, but also enables the phenomenologist to investigate the non-phenomenality of other persons. That is, a Levinasian *epoché* must allow the other person to give her- or himself to the one performing the *epoché* as someone whose meaningfulness is not initially, and for the most part, constituted by the performer of the *epoché*. *I will call this Levinasian epoché the ethical epoché.*[27]

This section aims to delineate the outlines of a Levinasian ethical *epoché*, modeled after the ethical reduction that Levinas himself performs in the second and third sections of *Totality and Infinity* and *Otherwise than Being*. More specifically, it will describe this ethical reduction in temporal terms so we will be in a position to properly critique Royce's temporalism from a Levinasian standpoint.

Revelation of the Face in Totality and Infinity

Horrified at the systematic violence committed against millions of persons by totalitarian regimes, which are the political embodiment of the logic of totality, in the twentieth-century, Levinas investigates how other persons reveal themselves to us beyond the logic of totality in *Totality and Infinity*.[28] Since he equates history with totality and assimilative violence,[29] he attempts to imagine a sense of interpersonal time when persons encounter one another non-simultaneously, that is, a non-historical time which places us in a position to judge history.[30] This non-historical time is ethical time; it is the time when others have the opportunity to testify to me and demand that I respect their irreducible singularity. In other words, this time is when other persons call me to be responsible for their welfare and, most importantly, not murder them, and the time where "[m]y being is produced in producing itself before the others in discourse."[31] Non-historical time is when I witness to others and expose myself to them as a fellow person worthy of not being subjected to violence.[32] In short, non-historical time is the time of justice.

Of course, Levinas's notion of ethical time has some important consequences for contemporary political philosophy; however, it is beyond the purview of this paper to investigate the political ramifications of Levinas's notion of ethical time.[33]

With that said, we are in a better position to appreciate why Levinas attempts to describe, phenomenologically, how the other person gives herself to us beyond the noetic-noematic structure of Husserlian intentionality, as articulated in Husserl's *Fifth Cartesian Meditation*.[34] Unlike Husserl—who conceives of the other person as either an alter ego, whose meaningfulness is constituted through our acts of empathy, or someone who is analogically appresented to us as inaccessible, or alien, to ourselves[35]—Levinas thinks that there is an additional and more originary sense in which the other person gives himself or herself to us. He calls this more originary source of the Other's self-revealing, "revelation,"[36] in *Totality and Infinity*. Otherwise phenomenology remains trapped with the logic of totality and participates in a transcendental solipsism where everything alien is converted into something familiar, even if such a conversion negates the alien's alterity. This conversion of the alien into the familiar is the movement Levinas calls *totality*.[37] Moreover, all phenomenological investigations of human experience that do not move beyond an investigation of phenomenality, then, are in danger of committing violence against others.

Without recourse to anything transcending phenomenality, there is nothing beyond being mastered, or at least potentially mastered, by the I as transcendental I (or, in the early Martin Heidegger's case, the I as *Dasein*) and assimilated into an often violent, monolithic totality. In that case human persons would really be the measure of all things, including the worth of other human persons' lives. Fortunately for us, Levinas thinks we have an experience of something transcending phenomenality: the face of the Other.

Given Levinas's concerns about the dangers of totality, we could interpret Levinas's ethical *epoché* in *Totality and Infinity* as an effort to examine how the other person gives herself beyond phenomenality in the mode of (ethical) revelation. A fruitful way to describe Levinas's ethical reduction is to emphasize the temporal dimension of the face-to-face encounter with the Other *qua* other person. However, in order to describe the interpersonal sense of time involved in the face-to-face encounter with the Other, we first must describe the self-enclosed proto-temporality of the I prior to this ethical encounter.

Up to this point, we have intimated that the I's narcissism is counter to and incompatible with the other-orientedness of the face-to-face encounter with the other person, but this characterization of the Same is only partially true. The Same *is* detrimental to the ethical, but only to the extent that living in the Same forces us to deny someone else's uniqueness and consider him or her an object that can be done with as we please. Yet there is a sense in which the Same is the prerequisite for us to enter into the ethical encounter with the Other. The Same prepares the way for genuine time, namely, interpersonal time.

The Same is the realm where we enjoy things in the world; it is the realm of sometimes healthy egoism. Seen phenomenologically, Levinas thinks that the primary relation we have to things is not an instrumental one, but one of enjoyment.[38] The things that we enjoy nourish and even constitute us.[39] Accordingly, they sustain us beyond the level of mere existence:

> Nourishment, as a means of invigoration, is the transmutation of the other into the same, which is in the essence of enjoyment: an energy that is other, recognized as other, recognized . . . as sustaining the very act that is directed upon it, becomes, in enjoyment, my own energy, my strength, me.[40]

Hence we somehow carve out a separate, autonomous space for ourselves through our acts of appropriating other things into ourselves, whether that appropriation manifests itself in our consumption of a delicious New York steak or in our appreciation of an artwork. For example, we do not eat to live, even though it is the case that eating is necessary for us to live. Rather, we eat because we enjoy what we are eating.[41] To do otherwise would be to reduce life to being merely the continuation of one's bare existence.

Enjoyment is nearly a catch-all notion for Levinas's sense; it is very similar, if not identical, to a classical Epicurean hedonism that does not necessarily imply libertinism or licentiousness. And we feel the sting of pain, the agony of suffering, and disappointment of enjoyment lost only because the initial sense of life is one of enjoyment and the pursuit of contentment.[42] What this means is that my life is actually a series of enjoyments consummated or denied, fulfilled or thwarted and frustrated.[43] This is the life of the Same where to exist as an I "means neither to oppose nor to represent something to itself, nor to use something, nor to aspire to something, but to enjoy something."[44]

In addition, as I enjoy the world, a world existing prior to me and that nourishes me, I live an earthly life—namely, the life of a situated creature that habituates itself in a sensible world—before I represent the world to myself.[45] This means that I enjoy and sense things in the world prior to representing these things to myself. In addition, by enjoying the world, I dwell in it intimately and feel at home in it.[46]

Yet, we do more than enjoy the world. We also live a life of intentionality. When we are consciously intending something, it acquires a meaning beyond the sensuous enjoyment that we experience when we simply consume it; in short, it becomes intelligible and thus available to us latter, at least in the form of a remembered object. Furthermore, the intelligibility of the now intended object makes us forgetful of its alterity. Moreover, every intentional act is bound to the present moment. In fact, whenever we intend something and represent it to ourselves—whether it be a memory of a previously consummated experience, a present enjoyment, or an anticipated experience—we do so within what Husserl calls the living present. This is experienced as an indefinite present, for there is no experience of temporal lapse in our acts of intending noema.[47] Seen phenomenologically, the I cannot intend anything beyond the present instant and experiences the passage of time as a series of present instants.[48] This solipsism of the present exhausts the self-temporalization of the Same. In other words, intending things in the world places us in a perpetual living present from which we cannot escape.

Nevertheless, we are more than persons who represent and recollect things in the world to ourselves in a perpetual series of present instants. Even in our non-natural acts of representing the world, we cannot negate completely the meaningfulness of what is exterior to us. As living, embodied creatures we cannot help but recognize that there is a meaningfulness to things in the world and other persons that we do not constitute, but is recognized by us as being meaningful.[49] Indeed, the irreducible alterity of things and other persons is what leads us to be sensitive to their exteriority. Encountering the exteriority of things and persons is not always violent, and thus detrimental to the comforting, intimate sense of being at home in the world. Sometimes encountering the undeniable alterity of things and, more importantly, the alterity of the other person, is even a gentle event.[50] Still, this initial exposure to the Other's alterity is not yet the face-to-face encounter with the Other.

In the face-to-face encounter with the Other, he or she "presents" herself or himself to us in its resistance to every effort of ours to negate her or his absolute alterity. However, the elusiveness of the Other's face is not a negative one, but one indicating its overflowing, non-phenomenal positivity. The Other gives herself to us in such a way that we are awakened from our egological slumber with her transcendence. This transcendence is not simply the transcendence associated with the object of our intentional act, rather it is similar to the one Gabriel Marcel describes in *Tragic Wisdom and Beyond*:

> There is an order where the subject finds himself in the presence of something entirely beyond his grasp. I would add that if the word "transcendent" has any meaning it is here—it designates the absolute, unbridgeable chasm yawning between the subject and being, insofar as being evades every attempt to pin it down.[51]

Of course, Levinas would strongly disagree with Marcel's elevation of ontology to the level of exemplifying transcendence. Yet, if we replaced Marcel's *being* with Levinas's *face of the Other*, we would have an apt description of how Levinas conceives of our experience of the Other. We could rephrase Marcel's point in Levinasian language. This revised point could be articulated along these lines. There is an order where I find myself solicited by something entirely beyond my grasp.

If the word "transcendent" has any meaning it is here; it designates the absolute, unbridgeable chasm yawning between me and the other person, insofar as the other person evades every attempt to convert her into a species of the Same.

Ironically, the Other's transcendence allows the concrete other person to give him- or herself to us as an epiphany in which we recognize that the Other appeals to us beyond his or her phenomenality.[52] We respond to the Other's revelation; we welcome the Other *as absolutely other*.[53] The Other is revealed to me as the one who appeals to me in a voice that inaudibly utters the biblical commandment "Thou shall not murder."[54] The Other speaks to me, then, first and foremost in an ethical voice, a voice that demands me to be responsible for her and, more importantly, not murder her. Encountering the Other, then, calls us to live up to our obligation to tend to our fellow persons' material needs, spiritual necessities, psychological well-being.[55]

While I admire Levinas's struggle to articulate how a non-phenomenal face speaks to me prior to physical gestures and audible linguistic signs, let me describe the non-phenomenal speech of the Other in more explicitly temporal terms. For the most part, I live within a relatively self-enclosed living present. I enjoy the world and am at home in it. Living life this way means that there is nothing absolutely alien to me. Whatever seems alien I impose some sort of familiar meaning onto it; that is, I somehow fit it within my world so that I still have a sense of being at home in the world.

Suddenly, without warning, I encounter the face of the Other. This face is not corporeal, wrapped in the mask of phenomenality. Here I experience something that I can neither fit within the Same nor deny its alterity. Additionally, I experience someone who has his or her own temporality; thus, I encounter someone who lives beyond the confines of my living present. This Other, who has a temporality not quite like my own, calls me to recognize him or her beyond his or her phenomenal features, and respect his or her radical alterity. Respecting another's alterity, in turn, allows us to dialogue with that person without reducing him or her to the Same.

Along the way the illusion of our dwelling in a perpetual living present vanishes. We come to recognize that we always already participate in an interpersonal world. This interpersonal world is one where we live with one another beyond the violence of history and the logic of totality. In this world, we live humbly before the Other, and everything else derives its meaning from our initial, pre-phenomenal encounter with the Other.[56]

Furthermore, ethical encounter is temporally prior to phenomenal experience because the face-to-face encounter solicits me, in the etymological sense of the Latin *sollicitare* (i.e., to shake or disrupt the totality),[57] out of my narcissistic solitude and live in an asymmetric, diachronic time with the Other.[58] Indeed, I cannot live a genuine temporal existence unless I first encounter the Other. Such a diachronic ethical time also reveals to us a messianic time where the promise of a future where divine justice will reign is ever-deferred. Yet, this ethical sense of the future motivates us to walk humbly with one another before the divine.[59] This is what Levinas means when he says that metaphysics precedes ontology.

There is at least one significant problem with Levinas's *epoché* in *Totality and Infinity*, however, which Bettina Bergo identifies in her criticism of it for basing "the experience of ethical temporality upon the dialectic of *eros*, fecundity, paternity and filiality."[60] The problem with him grounding his notion of ethical time on these non-ethical senses of interpersonal alterity, especially on intergenerational fecundity,[61] is that they are not able to be articulated within a Levinasian ethical reduction, at least as performed by Levinas in *Totality and Infinity*.

In the cases of fecundity and paternity, a Levinasian *epoché* cannot describe them adequately due to it being a mostly static phenomenological analysis of the face. And even when a Levinasian *epoché* does engage in a genetic phenomenological analysis, it concentrates almost exclusively on how we develop into autonomous individuals, not on how the interpersonal, face-to-face encounter unfolds temporally. At most Levinas describes the temporal sense of the face-to-face encounter with the Other vaguely and implicitly. In short, a Levinasian ethical reduction, as performed in *Totality and Infinity*, cannot base our interpersonal ethical temporality on fecundity and filiality because it does not perform the generative analysis[62] of these senses of interpersonal alterity necessary to base our interpersonal ethical temporality on such non-ethical, intergenerational "phenomena."

Ethical Temporality in Otherwise than Being

In *Otherwise than Being* Levinas corrects his earlier mistake in *Totality and Infinity* and bases ethical temporality on our encounter with the Other. This methodological adjustment to his ethical reduction enables him to articulate adequately the ethical temporality of the interpersonal encounter with the Other, since it places him in the position to examine phenomenologically how ethical time is dependent on the disturbance of our own self-temporalization. Indeed, any adequate description of ethical temporality has to critique successfully Husserl's persuasive phenomenological description of self-temporalization in his analyses of internal time consciousness. This is so because Levinas thinks that Husserl's internal time consciousness is actually an adequate description of how the I experiences time.

Concerning the temporal existence of the I (*moi*), Levinas writes in Husserlian fashion:

> In [the I's] temporalization, in which, thanks to retention, memory, and history, nothing is lost, everything is presented or represented, everything is cosigned and lends itself to inscription, or is synthesized or, as Heidegger would say, assembled, in which everything is crystallized or sclerosized into substance—in the recuperation temporalization, without time lost, without time to lose, and where the being of substance comes to pass.[63]

Here Levinas describes the time of intentionality, or, better yet, how intentionality constitutes the I's temporality. Being conscious of something is a temporalization of the I in the sense that whatever the I is conscious of, it takes time to accomplish the intentional act. Yet, this duration does not allow any mode of temporality to enter into consciousness that disrupts the perpetual, ageless flow of the living present.[64] As we noted earlier, intentionality occurs in a seemingly absolute present, a perpetually extending and self-enclosed present instant. That is, self-temporalization is not able to conceive of a genuine temporal movement, where the I moves and has its being among other temporalities not reducible to its own. All time, then, is held or intended within the orbit of the I's self-temporalization.

Unfortunately, the I's self-temporalization falsifies time by covering over the non-recoupable lapses of time that constitute the passage of time. It is only when the Other approaches me that I, as a self (*soi*), sense a time that is non-representable to me in my present, a time beyond my living present. That is, it is only when we are affected sensibly by the non-assimilable alterity of the Other, which unmasks the works of consciousness and its attempt to construct an absolute and continuous time, that we are able to live in genuine (ethical) time. What this means is that it is only in proximity to the Other, when the Other's face accuses me of narcissistic self-indulgence and calls me to be responsible for the Other, that I am able to have time.

Given Levinas's ethical reduction in *Otherwise than Being*, we could describe the three modalities of time along these lines. Initially, and for the most part, we dwell in the living present. In fact, left to ourselves we could not escape the solipsism of the living present. We awaken from the living present only in the presence of that which is non-representable, but takes me hostage. This means that we awaken from the slumber of the living present only when we are affected by illeity, which "overflows both cognition and the enigma through which the Infinite leaves a trace in cognition."[65]

We experience illeity as the ever-receding, immemorial past where the Other calls me to be responsible for him or her, but is never present to me as a phenomenon.[66] We could think of illeity as the originary source

> for the order to come from I know not where, this coming that is not a recalling, is not the return of a present modified or aged into a past, this non-phenomenality of the order, which, beyond representation affects me unbeknownst to myself, "slipping into me like a thief."[67]

Being affected by the trace of illeity is an experience of passivity that is more passive than that of kinesthetic passive syntheses. This non-phenomenal, experiential reception of the pre-originary givenness of the Other is more passive than kinesthetic passive syntheses because the latter's passivity is still an act of sense-constitution, however receptive they are to the noema that affects the body on a precognitive level.[68] Moreover, this pre-originary givenness is felt as a trauma and a persecution; it is felt viscerally as an exposed vulnerability to an alien force; a suffering; a pain; an absolute passivity at the accusative face.

A simplistic way of illustrating the visceral quality of our encounter with the Other's face is to say that the affective lure of the Other's face on the non-phenomenal level is analogous to the affective lure of sensed things on the phenomenal level.[69] Yet unlike the affective lure of sensed things, which are present to us as intended objects, the face of the Other is never present to us. As we approach the Other, the neighbor for whom we are responsible, the Other recedes into a past prior to any past that we could ever remember; that is, any past that could be the object of intentional memory. What is left is an obligation, an immemorial ethical imperative binding me to other persons, that I never had an opportunity to decide whether or not to accept as my own, yet is one that commands me to be responsible for the Other.

While *Otherwise than Being* does not concentrate on the futural dimension of ethical temporality, Levinas still seems to conceive of ethical futurity in terms of the messianic time intimated toward the end of *Totality and Infinity*. In a conversation occurring at the University of Leyden on March 20, 1975,[70] Levinas says that his notion of messianic future in *Totality and Infinity* is compatible with his notion of the immemorial past in *Otherwise than Being*. Such a future is "a patient waiting for God . . . but a waiting without an awaited."[71] That is, like the immemorial past, messianic time stretches into the indefinite future like an ever-deferred promise. Consequently, the future of ethical temporality is not an anticipation of a definite future; rather, "it is unknown from the outset."[72]

In his 1982 article "Diachrony and Representation,"[73] Levinas further describes the sense that futurity has in ethical temporality:

> There is in the Other a meaning and an obligation that oblige me beyond my death! The futuration of the future does not reach me as a to-come [à-venir], as the horizon of my anticipations or protentions. . . . Responsibility for the Other, responding to the Other's death, vows itself to an alterity that is no longer within the province of re-presentation. This way of being avowed—or this devotion—is time.[74]

Viewed from the vantage point of ethical temporality, the future is not yet an actual event, but a vow to be responsible for the Other even unto death. As such, this vow is eschatological in nature. Such an ever-deferred future has an affective lure on us and serves as the originary condition for the possibility of us living in a less violent future. And like the immemorial past, the ethical future is an intrusion into the violence of history and serves as the condition for the possibility of non-violent, ethical events to occur in the midst of our concrete, empirical world.

A Levinasian Critique of Royce's Temporalism

We are now prepared to critique Royce's temporalism from a Levinasian standpoint. The problem with Royce's temporalism is that it is too egological. Indeed, Royce's notion of internal time-consciousness depicts us as ethical selves who consider other persons as meaningful only insofar as they are related to that self's life-plan. This holds true however structurally prior intersubjectivity happens to be in the initial constitution of that self's subjectivity (and, by extension, one's sense of temporality) and however altruistic that self's life-plan might be. Even when we encounter other human persons who have their own unique temporalities, there is a strong probability that we will consider them simply as alter egos,[75] and thus regard them as being meaningful not in themselves, but only insofar as they are assimilated into our own subjectivity. In this case, the other person ceases to be genuinely Other and becomes merely another "construct" of ours.

This, in turn, leads us dangerously close to denying our responsibility to live by any immemorial ethical imperative, since such a self-enclosed subjectivity precludes the possibility for anyone to have any significance beyond whatever meaning we happen to confer on her or him.

Luckily, Levinas offers us an alternative to Royce's egological view of human temporality. Instead of describing our temporality as originating from our self-constituting subjectivity, specifically its internal time-consciousness, Levinas's ethical *epoché* enables us to see that our sense of time originates from our face-to-face encounters with other persons. This means that we cannot simply regard other persons as alter egos who have significance for us only insofar as they are contemporaneous with us, that is, insofar as they exist simultaneously in the *same* temporal horizon that we do.[76] This also means that we do not literally or figuratively live in the same (experiential) time with anyone else, or as the title of one of Gabriel Marcel's dramas says, "My Time Is Not Yours" (*Mon temps n'est pas le Votre*).

Yet, Levinas's phenomenology does not leave us with an utterly fragmented world, inhabited by self-enclosed temporalities with absolutely no means of relating to one another. Rather he thinks that once we have escaped from our tendency to view being-in-the-world through our normal egological standpoint, we become receptive to how we initially encounter other persons diachronically and how our own subjectivity acquires its significance in such discontinuous face-to-face encounters. In turn, this diachrony of experiential time binds us to an immemorial ethical imperative that we are responsible to obey, without us ever having a choice in the matter or the ability to abnegate our responsibility to obey it. This ethical imperative, as we stated earlier in this section, originates whenever we encounter what Levinas calls the face of the Other.[77] Encountering the face of the Other reminds us that we have an obligation "to cede [our] place in the sun," as Pascal would say, to the other person, whoever that person may be, and tend to her unique material needs, spiritual necessities, and psychological well-being.[78]

Levinas demands that we acknowledge the difficult truth that to be genuinely ethical means to act counter to our natural egological dispositions, and he reminds us that we are responsible for the Other, regardless of whether or not we choose to act responsibly toward him or her. Once we encounter the Other, we ought to recognize immediately that we are ethically obligated to protect, persevere, and cherish her to the best of our abilities. To be genuinely ethical, then, is to willingly assume our always already existent responsibilities to the Other, which include us acting to promote other persons' material, psychological, emotional and spiritual welfare without expecting anything in return from them and without negating their alterity.

This means that for us to have this sort of relationship with the Other, we have to be able to be genuinely receptive to our fellow persons, which means that we let them reveal themselves to us as more than merely alter egos; it means that we see them as fellow *moral* persons deserving of our hospitality and ethical consideration. Of course, such a revelatory givenness is viewed from our natural egological standpoint as a perpetual intrusion, disturbance, or interruption of our self-constituted temporality.[79] Yet, this apparently disruptive mode of givenness is, in fact, the basis for an intersubjective, experiential time that is non-egological, or at least not initially constituted by the subject alone. Practically speaking, this means that the actual encounters we have or might have with others—e.g., Malcolm opening a door for an elderly person—are among the innumerable concrete circumstances that constitute our temporality. And even when we unjustly discriminate against another person, it is a circumstance that contributes to the intersubjective constitution of time, despite the fact that such an act denies our ethical obligation to the Other.

Royce's Temporalism Coupled with Levinasian Insights

Let us end this chapter by explaining why I think Royce's temporalism would profit from incorporating the above insights from Levinas's phenomenology. I think that coupling Royce's temporalism with Levinas's intersubjective ethical theory of time would allow it to discuss the ethical dimension of human temporality in a non-egological manner, or at least not base its descriptions of human temporality on an egological standpoint. That is, incorporating such a phenomenological description of the ethicality of human temporality into Royce's temporalism would enable us to appreciate how our encounters, interactions, and relationships with other persons are initially experienced as interruptions of our egological standpoint and would force us to recognize how our sense of temporality is primordially constituted by our encounters with other persons.

For those persons who would contend that Royce's temporalism does address how our temporality is constituted by our encounters with others in such works as *The Problem of Christianity*, I would remind them that even in *The Problem of Christianity* he does not directly examine how ethical intersubjective time is structurally prior to our egological temporality. This is a noticeable and damning oversight on Royce's part; however, it is one that a Roycean temporalism can overcome by incorporating a Levinasian phenomenological approach into its own approach.

Lastly, what would a Roycean temporalism that has integrated a Levinasian description of human temporality into its own look like? It might resemble the following account of human temporality.

While we naturally consider the origin of our sense of time to be our internal time-consciousness, when we engage in an in-depth phenomenological analysis of our temporality, we recognize that it originates not in our internal time-consciousness, but in our encounters with other persons. However, these encounters with other persons are pre-cognitive and pre-perceptual; they serve as the condition for the possibility of our having any sense of temporality at all. This means that without us being receptive to other persons, we are trapped within the solipsism of our egological standpoint.

Upon further phenomenological reflection on the intersubjectivity of human temporality, we realize that our encounters with other persons presuppose that there is an ethical dimension to each and every encounter. Accordingly, our temporality derives its meaning from our encounters with other persons, or more specifically, from our response to an ethical imperative that has called us since time immemorial, an ethical imperative that expresses itself in the face of the concrete Other. This ethical imperative, then, demands that we live for-the-other and tend to his or her material, psychological, and spiritual needs and interests whenever we have the means to do so. Moreover, we are expected to be exemplars of this ethical imperative by assuming responsibility for-the-other, even if no one reciprocates our acts of non-egological altruism.

Hopefully, our non-egological acts of altruism will help create communities that try to actualize the ideal of the Beloved Community to the utmost of their ability, even though it is beyond their (and our) capacity to actualize fully. Indeed, the ideal of the Beloved Community could be interpreted as being synonymous with, if not identical to, this immemorial ethical imperative. Our responses to this ethical imperative once we initially encounter others constitute our temporality in the most originary sense.

CLOSING REMARKS

Let me end this book where I began it. In the Introduction, I announced that this book is an apparent hodgepodge of philosophical topics, methods of argumentation, and exegesis. Then, I offered a concise paragraph describing how the chapters of this book hang together as a single philosophical work. Nonetheless, I did not tell the reader *what* precisely unifies my inquiries into a single work in the Introduction. I gave an intimation of what makes this book a unified whole in the last paragraph or so of my Preface. In it I described this book as the result of a years-long encounter with Royce's ethico-religious insight. Indeed, what unifies the diverse investigations conducted in this book is that every one of them is a chronicle of my encounter with Royce's ethico-religious insight. I know that a standard philosophy text would probably have stated this unifying theme in the opening paragraphs of the Preface or the Introduction. I decided against announcing the unifying theme in advance in order to have readers encounter Royce for themselves.

What is there left to write? I personally think that it would be a waste of time summarizing how I have encountered Royce's ethico-religious insight in reading him as an American personalist, interlocutor to Martin Luther King, Jr., and ethicist who needs Levinas's ethical metaphysics to have his ethical thought live up to its potential. The previous chapters should have clarified for readers how I have encountered Royce's ethico-religious insight in these ways.

So where does this leave me? Convention frowns upon an author introducing new material at the conclusion of his or her work. However, I would like to end this book with a more recent encounter I have had with Royce's ethico-religious insight.[1] Royce has been touted recently as one of the earliest professional American philosophers to grapple with the issues of racism in American society, particularly racism against the Japanese, Asian Americans, and African Americans in the late nineteenth and early twentieth centuries.[2] He has even been interpreted as advancing an anti-essentialist conception of race.[3] That is, Royce is read as conceiving of racial identities in terms of contingent, historical circumstances, and not of biological necessity. Racial groups are formed due to intergenerational patterns of cultural practice, societal norms, and similar historical situatedness. These interpreters of Royce think that this is how he is able to write such passages as this:

> The Germanic ancestors of the present western Europeans were barbarians, although of a high type. But when they met civilization, they first adopted, and then improved it. Not so was it with the Indians, with the Polynesians. Here, then, is the test of a true mental difference amongst races. Watch them when they meet civilization. Do they show themselves first teachable and then originative? Then they are mentally higher races. Do they stagnate or die out in the presence of civilization? Then they are of the lower types. Such differences, you will say, are deep and ineradicable, like the differences between the higher and lower sorts of individual men. And such difference will enable us to define racial types of mind. I fully agree that this test is an important one. Unfortunately, the test has never been so fairly applied by the civilized nations of men that it can give us any exact results.[4]

At the end of "Race Questions and Prejudices," however, he contends that we should consider ourselves, first and foremost, to be members of a single human race who happen to live in different local and regional communities, some of which are organized around racial identities.[5] So far, so good.

Nevertheless, Royce seems to have espoused a racism against black persons based not on inherent biological inferiority, but on cultural and intellectual inferiority. His example of how the English colonizers of Jamaica introduced "civilization," in the form of bureaucratic administration and technocratic order, to the people of African descent residing there is an example of the sort of racism common in contemporary America. Royce's association of Jamaican blacks with culturally inferior persons can be understood as an early example of what some social scientists call laissez-faire racism, an idea that Lawrence Bobo, James Kluegel, and Ryan Smith characterize this way: "Laissez-faire [antiblack] racism involves persistent negative stereotyping of African Americans [and other persons of African descent], a tendency to blame blacks themselves for the black–white gap in socioeconomic standing, and resistance to meaningful policy efforts to ameliorate U.S. [and international] racist social conditions and institutions."[6]

Laissez-faire antiblack racism is normally the sort of racism that arose after the dismantlement of Jim Crow racism, namely, legalized institutional segregation and racial discrimination against African Americans.[7] Yet Royce's position on racism against African Americans appears to be a precursor to this sort of anti-essentialist racism. Like Royce, contemporary proponents of laissez-faire antiblack racism do not argue that African Americans are intrinsically inferior to Euro-Americans, but they do condone whatever institutionalized racial inequalities exist currently. Like Royce, they accept these institutionalized racial inequalities between African Americans and Euro-Americans because they think of African Americans as having inferior cultural and volitional practices (e.g., poor work ethic and a proclivity for criminal behavior), and that this explanation alone is sufficient to justify these existing inequalities.[8]

Unlike contemporary white antiblack racists, however, Royce lived in the era of Jim Crow segregation in the South and de facto segregation in the North. While he was alive, legal institutional forces and unjustly discriminatory prejudices operated to keep a majority of African Americans in subservient socioeconomic conditions. Yet, he judged the inferiority of African Americans (and other persons of African descent) on cultural and volitional factors, as though they could attain the material wealth and social status of bourgeois Euro-Americans just by adopting their cultural practices (for example, rigid bureaucratic administration of governmental affairs). Royce could not see how his unquestioning acceptance of detrimental antiblack stereotypes let him neglect the fact that persons of African descent belonged to millennia-old Afro-Muslim, Afro-Christian, and indigenous African civilizations, with the Afro-Muslim Moors ruling most of the Iberian Peninsula and much of southern Europe along the northern Mediterranean Sea for nearly 800 years.[9]

Of course, Royce would have learned a biased history of the ancient and modern worlds, where Greco-Roman civilization dominated southern Europe, North Africa, and the Near East between the fourth century B.C. and fifth century A.D. Moreover, he probably would have been taught that after nearly a millennium of cultural decline in Western Europe, Western societies rekindled their cultural and economic vitality by rooting itself in their classical, Greco-Roman past. He most likely would not have learned that Afro-Muslims and sub-Saharan Africans contributed to world civilization during the European Dark Ages. Nor would he have learned that European colonizers often encountered African societies that had far superior cultural practices and material wealth than they did. Ironically, it was precisely the very bureaucratic and technocratic mindset that Royce praised in the British colonizers that led European colonizers to colonize most of Africa and enslave millions upon millions of her native inhabitants.

His anti-essentialist antiblack racism is problematic for an additional reason: he admonishes Euro-American Southerners in early-twentieth-century America not to lynch African Americans not because they are persons who deserve respect and full citizenship, but because doing so would sully the moral dignity of the Euro-American Southerners. Even though "Race Questions and Prejudices" was an address given at a time when most Euro-Americans would have embraced antiblack racism, it does not justify Royce's use of the tropes of white superiority and black inferiority. Nor does it justify his elevation of European colonizers to a higher moral status than the colonized, as he did in the following passage where he tells his Southerner brothers how to nonviolently demonstrate their racial superiority by modeling the British approach to the Jamaican race problem:

> Be my superior quietly, simply showing your superiority with your deeds, and very likely I shall love you for the very fact of your superiority. For we all love our leaders. But tell me that I am your inferior, and then perhaps I may grow boyish, and may throw stones. Well, it is so with races. Grant then that yours is the superior race. Then you can afford to say little about the subject in your public dealings with the backward race. Superiority is best shown by good deeds and by few boasts.[10]

I cannot see how Royce's apparent racial anti-essentialism is an acceptable position, given that it seems to be a form of cultural antiblack racism. That is true even though many scholars of American philosophy have noted the progressive nature of his stance on the race question, remembering that Royce's position on this issue was actually progressive for his time in most intellectual Euro-American circles. I have not fully worked through the implications of his anti-essentialist racism for the validity of his ethico-religious insight. For example, I have yet to determine if his ethico-religious insight can be untangled from the taint of his apparent anti-essentialist, antiblack racism. For now, I read Royce's ethico-religious insight as a worthwhile contribution to American philosophy, and indeed to Western philosophy in general.

Notes

PREFACE

1. Frank M. Oppenheim, S.J., *Royce's Voyage Down Under* (Lexington: University Press of Kentucky, 1980), 25.

2. Some readers might wonder why I call Royce's idealism an "absolutistic idealism" rather than an "absolute idealism." I use the phrase "absolute idealism" to describe Hegel's idealism and its philosophical descendants, and Royce's idealism, contrary to popular opinion, is not any sort of Hegelian idealism (see *"Author's* Preface," in *Problem of Christianity* (1913) [Washington, DC: Catholic University of America Press, 2001], 39, where Royce denies any allegiance to Hegelian idealism). However, the absolute is at the heart of Royce's idealism, so I decided to call his idealism, "absolutistic idealism," to distinguish it from Hegelian absolute idealism.

3. The reasons why I turned away from Royce's absolutistic idealism are documented in my article "Concerning the God That Is Only a Concept: A Marcellian Critique of Royce's God," *Transactions of the Charles S. Peirce Society* 42.3 (Summer 2006): 394–416.

INTRODUCTION
ENCOUNTERING JOSIAH ROYCE'S ETHICO-RELIGIOUS INSIGHT

1. Josiah Royce, *Fugitive Essays*, ed. J. Loewenberg (1920) (Freeport, N.Y.: Books for Libraries Press, Inc., 1968), 9–10.

2. All of these essays are reprinted in ibid.

3. See James H. Cotton, *Royce on the Human Self* (Cambridge: Harvard University Press, 1954), quoted in *Josiah Royce's Late Writings: A Collection of Unpublished and Scattered Works*, vol. 1, ed. Frank M. Oppenheim, S.J. (Bristol, England: Thoemmes Press), 34.

4. All biblical citations are from *Zondervan KJV Study Bible* (Grand Rapids, Michigan: Zondervan, 2002) unless otherwise noted.

5. The literature on Royce's philosophy, especially dealing with his ethical thought and his philosophy of nature, has grown rapidly over the last few decades or so. A majority of this literature, though, attempts to describe Royce's philosophy in secular philosophical terms to fit more readily into contemporary philosophical conversations and to have more philosophers willing to examine Royce's thought. Here are a few examples of contemporary articles, essays, and books written by Royce scholars who engage in this practice: José-Antonio Orosco, "Cosmopolitan Loyalty and the Great Global Community: Royce's Globalization," in *Journal of Speculative Philosophy* 17.3 (2003): 204–15 and Griffin Trotter, *The Loyal Physician: Roycean Ethics and the Practice of Medicine* (Nashville: Vanderbilt University Press, 1997).

6. John Dewey, *A Common Faith*, in *Later Works of John Dewey*, vol. IX, ed. Jo Ann Boydston (Carbondale: Southern Illinois University Press, 1989), 1–60.

7. Rufus Burrow, Jr., *Personalism: A Critical Introduction* (St. Louis: Chalice Press, 1999).

CHAPTER ONE
THE "CONCEPTION OF GOD" DEBATE:
SETTING THE STAGE FOR ROYCE'S PERSONALISM

1. See Oppenheim, *Royce's Voyage Down Under*; he divides Royce's philosophical career into three periods: the early period (1883–95), middle period (1896–1911), and mature period (1912–16)—although in recent years he refers to this as his late period; I follow this designation.

2. I admit that Royce placed a tremendous amount of importance on logic in his philosophizing. He notes the importance of logic to philosophical inquiry as late as December 1915 in his informal "Autobiographical Sketch," given on the occasional of the American Philosophical Association's celebration of his sixtieth birthday (Josiah Royce, *The Basic Writings of Josiah Royce*, vol. I [Chicago: University of Chicago Press, 1969], 40). Yet there are already first-rate scholarly books documenting the importance of logic to Royce's thought. This book serves as a corrective to the tendency among many contemporary Royce scholars to emphasize his logic over his ethico-religious insight.

3. Josiah Royce initially referred to this omniscient and omni-benevolent judge as "Absolute Thought" in *The Religious Aspect of Philosophy* (1885) and later referred to this same judge as "Absolute Experience," in *The Conception of God* (1895). See Oppenheim, *Royce's Voyage Down Under: Royce's Mature Philosophy of Religion* (Notre Dame, Ind.: University of Notre Dame

Press, 1987) 18; and "High Points in Josiah Royce's Intellectual Development," in *Metaphysics*, ed. William Ernest Hocking, Richard Hocking, and Frank Oppenheim (Albany: State University of New York Press, 1998), xv, for more details concerning this initial insight in Royce's philosophical career.

4. I realize that in contemporary academic writing the usage of the third-person masculine pronouns and possessive pronoun is considered insensitive, inappropriate, and, at worst, outright offensive, even when someone is using them to refer to the divine. Nevertheless, since the acceptable alternatives to the third-person masculine pronouns and possessive pronoun would either portray the divine as an impersonal deity or cosmic process (it, its) or as a feminine deity (her, hers), both of which I want to avoid doing, I choose to revert back to the more traditional usage of "he," "him," and "his" to indicate the divine as personal. Please do not mistake my usage of the third-person masculine pronoun and possessive pronouns as me saying that God is male. What I am doing is reminding the reader that God is a personal spirit, not that God is a gendered being.

5. See "The Problem of Job," *Studies of Good and Evil* (1898), reprinted in *The Basic Writings of Josiah Royce*, vol. 2, ed. John J. McDermott (Chicago: University of Chicago Press, 1969). In his late writings, especially from *The Problem of Christianity* onward, Royce ceases to refer to this divine preserving function as "the Absolute" and instead refers to the divine as "Interpreter Spirit" or "Spirit" of the Beloved Community."

6. See Elizabeth Flower and Murray G. Murphey, eds., *A History of Philosophy in America* (New York: G. P. Putnam's Sons, 1977), vol. II.

7. For more on these aspects of Royce's philosophy, see Frank Oppenheim, *Royce's Mature Ethics* (Notre Dame, Ind.: University of Notre Dame Press, 1993).

8. See ibid.

9. Ibid., 19.

10. Ibid.

11. John Smith, *Royce's Social Infinite* (New York: Liberal Arts Press, 1950). Smith associated Royce's late thought with Peirce's philosophy that he calls Royce's metaphysics of community, a "metaphysics of interpretation."

12. Josiah Royce, *Problem of Christianity* (1913) (Washington, D.C.: Catholic University of America Press, 2001).

13. Gary L. Cesarz makes this point in "A World of Difference: The Royce-Howison Debate on the Conception of God," *Personalist Forum* 15.1 (Spring 1999): 126–27.

14. Randall E. Auxier, "Editor's Introduction," in *Critical Responses to Josiah Royce, 1885–1916* (Bristol, England: Thoemmes Press, 2000), vol. I, ix–x. Auxier has since altered his opinion to resemble the above position in his late writings on Royce's philosophy, especially Randall E. Auxier's "Josiah Royce," in *Dictionary of Modern American Philosophers*, ed. John R. Shook (Bristol, England: Thoemmes Press, 2005), vol. IV, 2089–96.

15. Randall E. Auxier, "Howison's and Hocking's Critique of Royce," *Personalist Forum* 15.1 (Spring 1999): 59–83, and his Introduction to *Critical Responses to Josiah Royce, 1885–1916*, vol. I.

16. Some Royce commentators, for example, John Clendenning and Vincent C. Punzo, conjecture that Howison criticized Royce's idealism as articulated in *The Religious Aspect of Philosophy* so relentlessly because of Howison's irritation at Royce for displacing him from his post at Harvard (see, e.g., John Clendenning, *Life and Thought of Josiah Royce*, rev.and expanded edition (Nashville: Vanderbilt University Press, 1999), 196, and Vincent C. Punzo, "*Royce on the Problem of Individuality,*" diss. St. Louis University, 1963, chap. 4, esp. pp. 134–35 note 1.

17. There has been some dispute over whether Borden Parker Bowne or George Holmes Howison was the first person to establish personalism—understood as the metaphysical position where "person" is the most significant metaphysical category and "persons" are the most real metaphysical entities—as a philosophical position in America. James McLachlan contends that George Holmes Howison was the first to establish "personalism" as a philosophical position in "George Holmes Howison: The Conception of God Debate and the Beginnings of Personal Idealism," *Personalist Forum* 11.1 (Spring 1995): 1–16, even though Borden Parker Bowne was the one who established an actual school of personalist thought, the Boston personalist tradition. Howison, in contrast, was never the head of any personalist school, despite the fact that Ralph Tyler Flewelling, Mary Whiton Calkins, and their respective personalisms were responses to Howison's idealism, and not Bowne's personalism. Also see Burrow, 41–42 and 54–56 for more on this dispute.

18. Ralph Tyler Flewelling, "George Holmes Howison: Prophet of Freedom," *Personalist* 38.1 (Winter 1957): 9.

19. George Holmes Howison coined the term "personal idealism" during "The Conception of God" debate in 1895 (McLachlan, "George Holmes Howison,"2).

20. Ibid., 5.

21. Ibid., 2.

22. See Flewelling, "George Holmes Howison," 7. McLachlan narrows the time span of Howison abandonment of Hegelianism and acceptance of personal idealism between 1892 and 1893.

23. Quoted in James McLachlan, "George Holmes Howison's 'The City of God and the True God as Its Head': The Royce-Howison Debate over the Idealist Conception of God," *Personalist Forum* 15.1 (Spring 1999): 9. McLachlan also refers to this quotation from Flewelling's "George Holmes Howison: Prophet of Freedom" in "George Holmes Howison," 8.

24. Flewelling, "George Holmes Howison," 10–11. Quoted in McLachlan, "George Holmes Howison," 6.

25. Ibid.

26. McLachlan, "George Holmes Howison," 5.

27. Ibid., 6.

28. These two essays are Stephen Tyman's "The Problem of Evil in the Royce-Howison Debate," *Personalist Forum* 13.2 (Fall 1997): 107–21 and McLachlan, "George Holmes Howison."

29. *Personalist Forum* 15.1 (Spring 1999).

30. Howison, *Conception of God*, x–xi.

31. McLachlan, "George Holmes Howison," 7. The quote in this passage is from Howison, *Conception of God*, xii.

32. McLachlan, "George Holmes Howison: 'City of God,'" 10–11, esp. 10, note 16.

33. Gabriel Marcel, *Royce's Metaphysics*, trans. Virginia Ringer and Gordon Ringer (Chicago: Henry Regnery Company, 1956), 23.

34. Ibid.

35. Ibid., 24–25.

36. Ibid., 24–25.

37. Ibid., 25. For a contemporary analytic philosopher's explanation of Royce's John–Thomas argument see Cesarz, "A World of Difference," esp. pp. 91–92.

38. Ibid.

39. Oppenheim, *Royce's Voyage Down Under*, 29–30.

40. Ibid., 25.

41. Ibid., 30.

42. Ibid., 88–89.

43. Ibid., 88.

44. See Cesarz, "Royce-Howison Debate," 108.

45. Josiah Royce, "The Conception of God," in *The Conception of God: A Philosophical Discussion Concerning the Nature of the Divine Idea as a De-*

monstrable Reality (1897), ed. George Holmes Howison, reprinted in *Critical Responses to Josiah Royce, 1885–1916*, ed. Randall E. Auxier (Bristol, England: Thoemmes Press, 2000), vol. I, 40–44.

46. Ibid., 43–44.
47. Ibid., 41.
48. Ibid., 47–48.
49. Ibid., 48.
50. Ibid.
51. Ibid., 49–50.
52. McLachlan, "George Holmes Howison, 'The City of God,'" 14, 27.

53. For a concise description of George Holmes Howison's personal idealism as he presented it in *The Conception of God*, see Stephen Tyman, "Problem of Evil in the Royce-Howison Debate," *Personalist Forum* 13.2 (Fall 1997): 111–16; McLachlan, "George Holmes Howsion,"9–12; and McLachlan, "George Holmes Howison's 'The City of God,'"13–17. For some description of Howison's mature pluralistic idealism see McLachlan, "George Holmes Howsion," 13–16; McLachlan, "George Holmes Howison's 'City of God,'" 18–26; Gary Cesarz, "Howison's Pluralistic Idealism: A Fifth Conception of Being?" *Personalist Forum* 15.1 (Spring 1999): 28–44; and, of course, George Holmes Howison's *The Limits of Evolution, and Other Essays Illustrating the Metaphysical Theory of Personal Idealism*, 2nd rev. and enlarged ed. (New York: Macmillan, 1904).

54. George Holmes Howison, "The City of God and the True God as Its Head," in *The Conception of God: A Philosophical Discussion Concerning the Nature of the Divine Idea as a Demonstrable Reality* (1897), ed. George Holmes Howison, reprinted in *Critical Responses to Josiah Royce, 1885–1916*, ed. Randall E. Auxier (Bristol, England: Thoemmes Press, 2000), vol. I, 98–99.

55. McLachlan, "George Holmes Howison," 9; Tyman, "Problem of Evil in the Royce-Howison Debate," 111.

56. Tyman, "Problem of Evil in the Royce-Howison Debate," 111.

57. I refer to this excerpt from McLachlan's "George Holmes Howison's 'City of God,'" 14, to flesh out Howison's criticism of Royce's arguments for his conception of God: "In his effort to leap over the abyss between subjective fragmentary knowledge and the Absolute, Royce fails to see that one could just as easily choose the solipsism of the individual knower as the reality of God. If the only choice is between solipsism and agnosticism, on one side, and belief in God or the Absolute on the other side, then—to the believer at least—the logic of the choice is irrelevant because it is not made

on logical but on moral and religious grounds. For Howison, the choice is ultimately a moral one not entailed by [the] formal logic of the argument."

58. Addressing whether an atheist can still be "loyal" to God, Royce writes the following in a July 23, 1904 letter to John Cotton Dana: "As to your views on 'godishness,' I doubt if you, after all, are so far away from idealism as you suppose. Some people veil their piety from themselves by a certain semblance of heresy, forgetting that the Absolute, if he exists, is the freest souled and most liberal and least petty or jealous minded or tyrannical of us all. One way to serve God is by doubting or even denying his existence, if only thereby you give your own faithfulness to ideal interests, and to truth, the clearest expression now possible to you. For faithful self-expression, with loyalty to ideal interests, is I take it, all that God means, for himself or for you; and so we don't disagree so much after all" (John Clendenning, ed. *The Letters of Josiah Royce* [Chicago and London: The University of Chicago Press, 1970], 477).

59. See Cornel West, "Pragmatism and Sense of the Tragic," reprinted in *The Cornel West Reader* (New York: Basic *Civitas* Books, 1999), 179.

60. Royce mentions on pp. 38–39 of the *"Author's* Preface" to *The Problem of Christianity* that at the height of his German idealist stage (1892–95) he was defined as more of a disciple of Schopenhauer than of Hegel or of any of the classical Hegelians. By 1913 he recognized that the formal structure of his work depended primarily on the work of C. S. Peirce.

61. One of the most compelling reconstructions of Royce's relational ontological argument appears in Cesarz, "A World of Difference," 93–128. In his reconstruction of Royce's argument, Cesarz demonstrates that Royce's relational ontological argument is an argument dependent on modal logic. I agree with Cesarz that Royce himself articulated his position by "appealing to a version of Aristotle's principle that possibility (or 'potentiality' in Aristotle's case) presupposes actuality, a principle that has since been found by many to be essential to modal logic and possible worlds theorizing" ("A World of Difference," 114). That is, we are only aware of possibilities as potentialities, or possible experiences embedded in actual experience. Yet, unlike Cesarz, Royce acknowledges that the possible is more than the realm of potentialities, but is the realm of genuine possibility: possibilities *qua* possibilities are dependent on the Absolute for their reality, but not on the Absolute as actuality, or a fully existent and completed process, as most traditional interpretations of Aristotle's philosophy would understand actuality. Possibility, in short, does not have to be actualized by the Absolute to be real. The Absolute only has to recognize that the possible is real for himself, and not ground the possible in the actual.

I would respond to Cesarz's comments on page 115 note 27 of "A World of Difference" thus: Royce did not ever recognize himself as a process philosopher, yet he places possibility *qua* possibility within the Absolute and lets Absolute Experience hold indeterminacies and possible experiences beyond any finite being (i.e., possibilities not tied to actual states of affairs) within himself. He even recognizes this truth on pp. 47–48 of *The Conception of God*. Royce did not realize until his encounter with Peirce's later logical writings that he understood pure actuality not in classical Aristotelian terms but more in terms of a Peircean Real; thus, the Absolute holds the totality of all possible and actual experiences within himself, and not that all real experience is reducible to actual (namely, spatio-temporally existent) experience. So Royce does embrace a central motif of process philosophy as early as 1895, and he develops this point further in his late philosophy.

Of course, this interpretation of Royce's position on possibilities heavily depends on his late metaphysics, as articulated in his 1915–16 Philosophy 9 Course on Metaphysics. This course has been published in William Ernest Hocking, Richard Hocking, and Frank Oppenheim, S. J., eds., *Metaphysics* (Albany: State University of New York Press, 1998). It is also present in his March 20, 1916, letter to Mary Whiton Calkins in which he describes the universe in terms of "Community" and "Spirit," both of which are growing and having an "endless fecundity of invention" (Clendenning, *Letters*, 644–45). By 1916, then, one can interpret Royce as saying that the universe is the concrete manifestation of a perpetually processing interpretation.

62. Oppenheim, *Royce's Voyage Down Under*, 25.

CHAPTER TWO
HAUNTED BY HOWISON'S CRITICISM:
THE BIRTH OF ROYCE'S LATE PHILOSOPHY

1. W. H. Werkmeister, *A History of Philosophical Ideas in America* (New York: Ronald Press Co., 1949), 134.

2. Ibid. During his years as an assistant professor of English at the University of California, Berkeley (1878—82), Royce wrote several essays emphasizing his voluntarism, most clearly in his essays on literary figures, for example, Robert Browning, and on ethics. For Royce's early voluntarism in ethics see "The Nature of Voluntary Progress" (1880) and "Tests of Right and Wrong" (1880) in *Fugitive Essays* (1920), Essay Index Reprint Series, ed. J. Loewenberg (Freeport, N.Y.: Books for Libraries Press, 1968), 96–132, 187–218.

3. Josiah Royce, "The Problem of Job," in *Studies of Good and Evil* (New York: D. Appleton, 1898), 1–28. This essay has been reprinted in *The Basic*

Writings of Josiah Royce, vol. II, ed. John J. McDermott (Chicago: University of Chicago Press, 1969).

4. Letter of Josiah Royce to William James, May 21, 1888, in *Letters of Josiah Royce*, ed. John Clendenning (Chicago: University of Chicago Press, 1970), 216.

5. Josiah Royce, "Physical Law and Freedom: The World of Description and the World of Appreciation," *Spirit of Modern Philosophy* (Boston: Houghton Mifflin, 1896), 381–434.

6. John J. McDermott, "The Confrontation between Royce and Howison," *Transactions of the Charles Peirce Society* 30.4 (Fall 1994): 788. Quoted in James McLachlan, "George Holmes Howison's 'The City of God and the True God as Its Head': The Royce–Howison Debate over the Idealist Conception of God." *Personalist Forum* 15.1 (Spring 1999): 8 note 8.

7. For examples of the palpable and felt experiences of evil and sufferings Royce had in his life see Frank M. Oppenheim, Sr., "Growing through Philosophy, Pain, and Prayer: Being Disciplined by Pain and Evil," in *Royce's Mature Philosophy of Religion*, 13–19, especially pp. 13–15.

8. Josiah Royce, "The Problem of Job," *The Basic Writings of Josiah Royce*, vol. II, 843. Stephen Tyman says that Royce articulated this point in *The Conception of God*. In it Royce "held the loving relationship between creator and creature to be fully reciprocal and fully experiential at the same time. Thus in the human person the Godhead itself dwells personally, longing in the longing of the individual and suffering in the individual's pain." Stephen Tyman, "The Problem of Evil in the Royce–Howison Debate," *Personalist Forum* 13.2 (Fall 1997): 113–14; Josiah Royce, "The Conception of God," in *The Conception of God: A Philosophical Discussion Concerning the Nature of the Divine Idea as a Demonstrable Reality*, ed. George Holmes Howison, in *Critical Responses to Josiah Royce, 1885–1916*, vol. I: *The Conception of God*, ed. Randall E. Auxier (Bristol, England: Thoemmes Press, 2000), 45–50. I agree with Tyman that this insight makes Royce a personalist.

9. Throughout this work I apply the anachronistic term "panentheism" (i.e., all-in-God) to Royce's philosophy. In its contemporary philosophical usage, the word was coined by Charles Hartshorne, a twentieth-century American process philosopher. However, one of the first Western idealist philosophers to advance panentheistic views is the German philosopher Karl Christian Friedrich Krause (1781–1832). Krause defines panentheism as "the view that what we can comprehend and imagine to be the universe, is an aspect of God, but that the being of God is in excess of this projection, and is neither identical with, nor exhausted by, the universe we can imagine and

comprehend." All subsequent Western panentheisms followed this general definition, including those of Hartshorne and, though not acknowledged, of Royce (Robert Wicks, "Arthur Schopenhauer," *Stanford Encyclopedia of Philosophy*, http://plato.stanford.edu/entries/schopenhauer/ [accessed June 16, 2008]). C. Alan Anderson and Deborah G. Whitehouse (*New Thought: A Practical American Spirituality* [New York: Crossroad Publishing Company, 1995], 89–92) quote Santiago Sia's explanation of panentheism from his *God in Process Thought* (Dordrecht: Martinus Nijhoff, 1985), as articulated by Hartshorne and as I apply to describe Royce's conception of the Divine: "Panentheism . . . holds that God includes the world. But it sets itself apart from pantheism in that it does not maintain that God and the world are identical. . . . Hartshorne explains that God is a whole whose whole-properties are distinct from the properties of the constituents. While this is true of every whole, it is more so of God as the supreme whole. . . . The part is distinguishable from the whole although within it. The power of the parts is something suffered by the whole, not enacted by it. The whole has properties too which are not shared by the parts. Similarly, God *as whole* possesses attributes which are not shared by his creatures. . . . We perpetually create content not only in ourselves but also in God. And this gives significance to our presence in this world."

10. On pages 98 and 99 of his essay "The City of God and the True God as Its Head." Howison attempts to equate Royce's conception of the Absolute with either the only actual entity in the universe, thus robbing us of any pretense of moral autonomy and individuality, or as solely a human construct that ultimately traps us in a radical solipsism. See Chapter 1 for an explanation of Royce's initial response to Howison's criticism.

11. Royce, "The Problem of Job," 844.

12. Ibid., 853.

13. Gabriel Marcel, *Royce's Metaphysics*, trans. Virginia Ringer and Gordon Ringer (Chicago: Henry Regnery Company, 1956), 27–28. For Royce, someone already knows the Real (i.e., the totality of beings in their relations with one another including the possibilities embedded in current states of affairs as well as the unrealized possibilities of the past and the not-yet possibilities of the future) in its entirety (at least up to the present moment) and will know the totality of the Real in the future. Marcel misses this point in the above excerpt, confusing Royce's conception of actuality, which refers to anything from past and presently existing beings to ideal or future beings, with the Aristotelian concept of actuality, which refers only to past and presently existing beings.

14. Josiah Royce, *Metaphysics*, ed. William Ernest Hocking, Richard Hocking, and Frank Oppenheim, S.J. (Albany: State University of New York Press, 1998).

15. Ibid. 78.

16. Loewenberg, "Editor's Introduction," *Fugitive Essays*, 23–24.

17. Royce, *Metaphysics*, 97–98. Royce seems to confuse at least momentarily "real" with "existent" on page 98 of *Metaphysics*. On that page he reverted back to one of the most common usages of "real" today: "occurring or existing in actuality" (Merriam-Webster's 11th Collegiate Dictionary, 2003).

18. On pages 237–42 of *Metaphysics*, Royce discusses possibility mostly in terms of potentiality, but he does allude to possibility *qua* possibility, which preserves the reality of possibilities not anchored in actual experience at all. William Ernest Hocking notices that Royce discusses the relation between the actual and the possible long before Alfred North Whitehead does: "Much illustration of possibility. As 'capacity,' it cannot be unreal. As 'freedom,' it is valid of human beings: they are their possibilities. (Long in advance of Whitehead, Royce emphasizes the importance of the category of possibility, whose puzzles had been brought out by Aristotle.)" (316 note 12).

19. Marcel, *Royce's Metaphysics*, 32.

20. I am grateful to Richard Beauchamp for introducing me to the phrase "locus of experience."

21. In this book I focus primarily on the function of purpose in the lives of minded beings. I do not mean, of course, that non-minded beings do not have any purpose whatsoever. However, since one of my central contentions in this book is that Royce's philosophy is an ethico-religious one, and Royce's ethics and philosophy of religion are human-centered.

22. Josiah Royce, "The Human Self," in *World and the Individual*, vol. II: *The Nature, Man, and the Moral Order* (New York: The Macmillan Co., 1901), reprinted in John E. Smith and William Kluback, eds., *Josiah Royce: Selected Writings* (New York: Paulist Press, 1988), 120–21.

23. Royce articulately expresses this "spiritual union of all persons" by each person acting in community, yet retaining their individuality, in Josiah Royce, *The Philosophy of Loyalty* (1908) (Nashville: Vanderbilt University Press, 1995). He further explains this spiritual union of all persons in his later works, *Sources of Religious Insight* (1912) (New York: Octagon Books, 1977) and *The Problem of Christianity* (1913).

24. In a December 2, 1909, letter to Agnes Boyle O'Reilly Hocking, Royce clarifies the non-causality of the Absolute as an Ideal and states that the Ab-

solute is not a causal power who enacts his will in the world from some supernatural perch, being metaphysically independent from all finite beings. In fact, to the extent that we consciously act to better the lives of our fellow persons (whether human or non-human), we act to actualize the ideal of an agapic community. This ideal of an agapic community is God in His futurity, in his future temporal modality.

25. Royce, "The Union of God and Man," in *World and the Individual* II, 418–25, 451–52.

26. Ibid., 452.

27. Royce discusses the purposive purposefulness of Nature itself in his *Metaphysics*. (Josiah Royce, *Metaphysics*, ed. William Ernest Hocking, Richard Hocking, and Frank Oppenheim [Albany: State University of New York Press, 1998]). In the stenographic transcript, Royce tells his students that according to his concrete and social idealism (i.e., his fourth conception of Being in the *World and the Individual*), "For idealism. . . . there is an intimate connection between essence and existence. For idealism, the reality of things consists in the fulfillment of certain purposes (109) . . . reality [is] the fulfillment of a purpose, an individual reality as the fulfillment of a purpose whereby a somewhat is distinguished from all others and from the world. This is in the end a super-social view of the nature of reality. A somewhat similar consideration appears to me to hold in the case of the identification of a physical object. That identification can be made only in purposive terms: what the thing is now is a further expression of the same idea or purpose whereby the thing was characterized, was distinguished from others in an earlier stage of experience" (153). In short, all beings—from subatomic particles to human organisms—are expressions of a purpose, of a tendency to fulfill particular ideals they try to actualize in their time-spans of actual existence. Royce, in a Peircean tone, tells us later in his *Metaphysics*, "To be is to signify something" (269). For every existent being, not to mention nonexistent but real beings (e.g., not-yet actualized ideals), its existence is the expression of a purpose which unifies all of its processes and encounters with other beings into a coherent identity.

28. See Royce, "Temporal and the Eternal." *The World and the Individual,* vol. II: *The Nature, Man, and the Moral Order*, 109–51.

29. I realize that some readers of the above paragraph might interpret certain portions of it as inconsistent with some of Royce's last writings concerning Germany during World War I, as his hawkish enthusiasm for America's entry into the war manifested itself in his public lectures as early as 1914, when most Americans still had grave reservations about entering the war.

His comments condemning Germany as an enemy of civilization in such venues as his Harvard lecture hall (see last lecture in *Metaphysics*) seem to contradict the spirit of his earlier ethical writings. However, Royce's often vehement condemnations of the entire German people do not negate his vision of the Beloved Community, even though they tarnish him as a person committed to the inclusive ideal of the Beloved Community and dedicated to respecting everyone as a member of a universal siblinghood. I discuss this topic in more depth in Chapter 5.

30. Griffin Trotter, *The Loyal Physician: Roycean Ethics and the Practice of Medicine* (Nashville: Vanderbilt University Press, 1997), 93.

31. Josiah Royce, *Philosophy of Loyalty*, 93.

32. Ralph Waldo Emerson, "Self-Reliance," in *Selections from Ralph Waldo Emerson: An Organic Anthology*, ed. Stephen E. Whicher (Boston: Houghton Mifflin, 1960), 153.

33. Edgar S. Brightman, *Moral Laws* (New York: Abingdon Press, 1933), 102.

34. Royce, *Philosophy of Loyalty*, 91–92.

35. Ibid., 53–54.

36. Ibid., 65.

37. Ibid., 160–61.

38. Ibid., 161–62.

39. In Royce's last major work, *The Problem of Christianity*, the term "Absolute" only appears three times in the index of Oppenheim's revised and expanded index of that work.

40. In fact, Royce says in *The Problem of Christianity*, "In spirit I believe my present book to be in essential harmony with the bases of the philosophical idealism set forth in various earlier volumes of my own, and especially in the work entitled 'The World and the Individual' (published in 1899–1901)" ("*Author's* Preface," 38).

41. Royce, *Sources of Religious Insight*, 160.

42. Ibid., 161.

43. Ibid., 160.

44. Ibid.

45. Ibid., 291–92.

46. Ibid., 204–10, 292.

CHAPTER THREE
ROYCE'S LATE PHILOSOPHY

1. This does not mean that my interpretation of Royce's *Problem of Christianity* is incompatible with more traditional interpretations of Royce's

masterwork that emphasize these conceptions. For more recent analyses of Royce's conceptions of atonement, redemption, and reconciliation, along with how they are related to his conception of the Beloved Community, see Jacquelyn Ann K. Kegley, "Grace, the Moral Gap, and Royce's Beloved Community," *Journal of Speculative Philosophy* 18.3 (2004): 171–83; Frank M. Oppenheim, S.J., *Reverence for the Relations of Life: Re-imagining Pragmatism via Josiah Royce's Interactions with Peirce, James, and Dewey* (Notre Dame, Ind.: University of Notre Dame Press, 2005), 422–23; and Kim Garchar, "Sin, Sorrow, and Suffering: A Graceful Response to the Deeper Tragedies of Life," Presentation at the 34th annual Society for the Advancement of American Philosophy, March 10, 2007.

2. Royce, *The Problem of Christianity*, 248–49.
3. Ibid., 261–62.
4. Ibid., 318–19.
5. I am indebted to Dwight Welch for introducing me to Henry Nelson Wieman's portrayal of God as being as real as a toothache in *The Wrestle of Religion with Truth* (New York: Macmillan, 1928), 2.
6. Royce, *The Problem of Christianity*, 268–70.
7. 1 Corinthians 12:12–14.
8. 1 Corinthians 13: 4–8.
9. Royce, *The Problem of Christianity*, 404.
10. Ibid, 402.
11. Ibid., 403–4.
12. Ibid.
13. Ibid., 399.
14. Cf. Josiah Royce, *Metaphysics*, 270–71.
15. Royce, *The Problem of Christianity*, 319, 362.
16. Ibid., 318–19.
17. Oppenheim, *Reverence for the Relations of Life*, 428.
18. Ibid.
19. In Royce's late philosophy he restricts his discussion of moral personhood to human beings. That does not mean that he automatically excludes any non-human organism from being a moral person.
20. Royce, *Problem of Christianity*, 254.
21. Several Royce scholars have written on Royce's appropriation of Peirce's semeiotics; see John E. Smith, *Royce's Social Infinite* (New York: The Liberal Arts Press, 1950) and John E. Smith, "Creativity in Royce's Philosophical Idealism," in *Contemporary Studies in Philosophical Idealism*, ed. John Howie and Thomas O. Buford (Cape Cod, Mass.: Claude Stark, 1975),

211–14; for this issue see also Griffin Trotter, *The Loyal Physician: Roycean Ethics and the Practice of Medicine* (Nashville: Vanderbilt University Press, 1997).

22. Oppenheim, *Royce's Mature Ethics*, 100.

23. Ibid.

24. Ibid., x.

25. Ibid., xiii. Royce discusses the notion of duty in the second lecture of his *1915–16 Extension Course on Ethics* in *Josiah Royce's Late Writings: A Collection of Unpublished and Scattered Works*, vol. 2, ed. and intro. Frank M. Oppenheim, S.J. (Bristol, England: Thoemmes Press, 2001) 77–92.

26. Ibid., xiii.

27. Ibid.

28. Ibid.

29. Ibid.

30. Oppenheim, *Royce's Mature Philosophy of Religion*, 35.

31. Whenever I mention such phrases as "felt experience," "lived experience," and "*felt, lived* historical process," I do not mean to imply that these experiences and phenomena are always passively received by a receptive organism, namely, the human self. I am using the terms "felt experience" and "lived experience" in a manner similar to Merleau-Ponty's usage of *vécu* in *corps vécu*—which is normally translated by English interpreters as the past participial "lived" in "lived body." In this context, "lived" is not a passively adjectival modifier of "body," but "implies some sort of awareness, even if prepredicative, that must be able somehow to grasp the 'being-in-the-world' of the lived body, as no feeling or activity confined to a merely physiological body could" (Errol E. Harris, *The Restitution of Metaphysics* [Amherst, N.Y.: Humanity Books, 2000], 3). I am inclined to agree with Harris that the "legitimate sense" of *vécu* in *corps vécu* is expressed in "the phrase . . . 'felt body,' or bodily feeling, and that does indeed include the whole content of consciousness (as Benedict Spinoza, G. W. F. Hegel, F. H. Bradley, and R. G. Collingwood [as well as Josiah Royce] were all well aware) . . ."; Ibid. This usage of "felt" and "lived" experience fits Royce's late conception of the person and his theory of interpretation because Royce does regard every act of interpretation as being a creative, novel, and dynamic act. But Royce focuses almost exclusively on the act of interpretation as a higher level cognitive and spiritual awareness done by an embodied minded being and neglects, for the most part, precognitive, physiological acts of interpretation done by our physical bodies (Royce, *The Problem of Christianity*, 290–91).

32. Oppenheim, *Royce's Mature Philosophy of Religion*, 34.

33. W. H. Werkmeister, *A History of Philosophical Ideas in America* (New York: Ronald Press, 1949).

34. For Howison's acknowledgment of the similarity between his pluralistic idealism and Royce's late idealism, read his essay "Josiah Royce: The Significance of His Work in Philosophy," in *Critical Responses to Josiah Royce, 1885–1916*, ed. Randall E. Auxier (Bristol, England: Thoemmes Press, 2000), vol. III, 11–12.

35. Howison, *The Limits of Evolution*, 352.

36. Ibid., 352 note 1.

37. Immanuel Kant, *Fundamental Principles of the Metaphysics of Morals*, trans. T. K. Abbott (Amherst, N.Y.: Prometheus Books, 1988), 58.

38. See Josiah Royce, "Immortality," in *William James and Other Essays on the Philosophy of Life*, Essay Index Reprint Series (Freeport, N.Y.: Books for Libraries Press, 1969), 257–98. The above interpretation of Royce's conception of immortality runs counter to the traditional interpretation advanced by Oppenheim: namely, that finite as I am, I must go on (after my biological death) in order to strive better to fill up my unique purpose in the universe. Oppenheim's interpretation presupposes that Royce's philosophy advances a version of subjective immortality. I contend that there is insufficient textual evidence for Oppenheim to interpret Royce's conception of immortality as a form of subjective immortality, at least in the essay in question.

39. The last work that Royce wrote prior to his death dealt with his notion of the cult of the dead. On page 7 of *Royce on the Human Self* (Cambridge: Harvard University Press, 1954), James H. Cotton quotes Royce's last manuscript in its entirety: "Amongst the motives that have made the religious life of humanity intense, endlessly disposed to renew its youth despite all of its disillusionments, and unfailingly precious, despite all of its changes and disappointments, is the motive expressed in one of the oldest and the newest of cults,—the cult of the dead. In this cult the most ancient people whose monuments are known to us join with the latest mourners who deplore, who commemorate, and who reverence their own lost ones. No one religious faith or practice, no limited range of beliefs regarding whether there is any human life after our bodily death, or regarding what such a life be, if there is one, can be justly regarded as invariably necessary in order that a genuine and vital cult of the dead should form a part of the religious experience of men. The most childlike of superstitions, as well as the deepest and the loftiest of man's efforts to read the mystery of his own life have contributed to the influence, have taken part in determining the importance of the

cult of the dead. This cult has survived countless changes of opinion. It will survive countless transformations of belief such as the future may have in store for us. Its spirit will grow.

"So long as love and memory and record and monument keep the thought of our own dead near to our lives and hearts, so long as patriotism and the spirit of human brotherhood enable us to prize what we owe to those who have lived and died for us, the cult of the dead will be an unfailing source to us of new and of genuinely religious life and . . . [text left uncompleted]." In this manuscript Royce remains loyal to his central ethico-religious insight unto death.

40. See Burrow, 53–66, where he classifies Howison's personal idealism, or what I call Howisonian personalism, as "teleological or ethical personalism."

41. Ibid., 64–65.

CHAPTER FOUR
ROYCE'S PERSONALISM

1. Thomas O. Burford, "What we are about?" *Personalist Forum* 1.1 (1985): 1. Available online at http://www.siu.edu/~tpf/Volume%201%20Web%20Files/Volume%201_1%20Editors%20Introduction.pdf (accessed July 25, 2008).

2. Ibid.

3. Erazim Kohak, quoted in Thomas Buford's "What we are about?" *Personalist Forum* 1.1 (1985): 2.

4. At this point, the reader might ask me, If Royce's philosophy had these similarities to Boston personalism, especially Bowne's personalism, then why did not Royce identify himself as a personalist? The likelihood of Royce using Bowne's term "personalism" to describe his philosophy would have been very slight, if not nonexistent, because Royce saw himself, first and foremost, as a neo-Kantian idealist in the mode of Lotze until late in his career, if he stopped interpreting his thought in that way at all. Second, personalism as a comprehensive philosophical system did not exist for most of Royce's career. Even though the term, in its contemporary philosophical usage, was introduced by Schleiermacher in 1799 and Charles B. Renouvier developed a sort of relational personalism in the late nineteenth century, personalism as a comprehensive philosophical system did not exist prior to Bowne christening his idealistic philosophy in 1908.

5. Erazim Kohak, "Personalism: Toward a Philosophical Delineation," *Personalist Forum* 13.1 (Spring 1997): 11. Yet Royce, in contrast with Kohak,

would assert that our acts of interpretation are inseparable from our personal experiences of the world; the act of interpretation is always personal even though the interpreter might not acknowledge the personal categories implicit in every act of interpretation.

6. Josiah Royce, *The Problem of Christianity* (Washington, D.C.: Catholic University of America Press, 2001 [1913]), 123.

7. See, for example, ibid.

8. Ibid.

9. Ibid., 268–69.

10. Ibid., 268.

11. Kohak, "Personalism," 11.

12. Rufus Burrow, Jr. "Borden Parker Bowne and the Dignity of Being." *Personalist Forum* 13.1 (Spring 1997): 45.

13. I described Royce's relational form of the ontological argument in Chapter 1 during my explication of his 1895 Berkeley address "The Conception of God." There I used the phrase "relational ontological argument" as a substitute for the phrase Royce used in *Metaphysics*, "relational form of the ontological argument."

14. Cf. Auxier, "Introduction," *Critical Responses to Josiah Royce,* v–x. Howison does recognize, though, that Royce's late idealism is different than his earlier idealism, and he even questions whether Royce remains an idealist after the publication of *The Problem of Christianity* and his writings on the epistemology of interpretation. However, he never understood Royce's panentheism and confused it with a Hegelian pantheism in 1895 and later with a Peircean pragmatism in 1916. See George Holmes Howison, "Josiah Royce: The Significance of His Work in Philosophy," in *Critical Responses to Josiah Royce, 1885–1916,* ed. Randall E. Auxier (Bristol, England: Thoemmes Press, 2000), vol. III, 3–16, esp. 11–13.

15. What I mean by the statement, "Royce's divine is Temporality itself," is that the divine's lived experience, namely the divine's experience of all temporal events at once while still experiencing the passage of each moment in its uniqueness, is the condition of possibility for the lived experience of each and every finite minded being. Here I call the divine's lived experience, "Temporality." I reserve the term "time" for the standardized measure of motion (e.g., clock time). See Chapters 5 and 7 below for a more detailed examination of what Royce means by "time" and "temporality," as I have defined it in this chapter.

16. Edgar S. Brightman, *Moral Laws* (New York: Abingdon Press, 1933), 79.

17. Burrow, *Personalism*, 35, 86.

18. Ibid., 35, 87. Royce would agree with this in an ethico-metaphysical sense. He would say that we are created to act spontaneously within the conditions of our situatedness in the world. Despite our situatedness, though, we have the potential to perform genuinely autonomous and novel acts; thus, we are metaphysically and ethically free. Royce also would agree with a Bownean notion of epistemic freedom either to analyze the world according to our fallible reason or to reject the conclusions of rational inquiry. Royce also agrees with Bowne that we are fitted to interpret events occurring in the world, faithfully, but would say that all of our interpretations are fallible and subject to revision. But Bowne would say the same, so there is no significant difference between Bowne and Royce on this point.

19. Ibid., 35,
20. Ibid., 35, 89.
21. Ibid., 102.
22. Ibid., 88.
23. Ibid.
24. Ibid., 88–89.
25. Griffin Trotter, *The Loyal Physician: Roycean Ethics and the Practice of Medicine* (Nashville and London: Vanderbilt University Press, 1997), 86–87.
26. Royce, *Problem of Christianity*, 361.
27. I thank Randall E. Auxier for getting me to take my position to its logical conclusion and for giving me helpful suggestions about how to do so.
28. The similarities between the Reverend Martin Luther King, Jr.'s personalism and Royce's personalism, especially their conception of the Beloved Community, are undeniable. Yet, the Roycean roots of King's Beloved Community are ignored, neglected, or otherwise not recognized by a vast majority of Royce and King scholars. Beyond a single paragraph in John J. Ansbro, *Martin Luther King, Jr.: The Making of a Mind* (1982), reprinted as *Martin Luther King, Jr.: Nonviolent Strategies and Tactics for Social Change* (Lanham, New York, and Oxford: Madison Books, 2000), 319 note 152, and Gary L. Herstein, "The Roycean Roots of the Beloved Community," unpublished manuscript. I am not aware of any literature on this topic written either by Royce scholars or King scholars.

Agreeing with Herstein's assessment of the Royce–King connection, I think that no Royce or King scholar could do anything other than give a plausible, circumstantial argument for the philosophical connection between Royce's and King's personalisms. See Herstein, "The Roycean Roots of the Beloved Community," for a plausible and persuasive argument for a Royce–King philosophical connection; for my association of Cornel West's prophetic pragmatism and Royce's personalism, read Rosemary Cowan's excellent work on West's thought, *Cornel West: The Politics of Redemption* (Malden, Mass.: Polity Press, 2003), esp. pp. 143–44, and compare her description of West's vision of humanity with Royce's metaphysics and ethics of community, as described in Part I of this text.

CHAPTER FIVE
ROYCE'S ETHICO-RELIGIOUS INSIGHT:
A HYPOTHETICAL POSTULATE?

1. Randall E. Auxier, "Josiah Royce" in *The Dictionary of Modern American Philosophers*, ed. John Shook (Bristol, England: Thoemmes Press, 2005) vol. IV, 2089–96.

2. See Randall E. Auxier, "Royce's Fictional Ontology," in *The Relevance of Royce*, ed. Kelly Parker and Jason M. Bell (New York: Fordham University Press, forthcoming). The papers in this volume were taken mainly from among those presented at the 2005 conference of the Josiah Royce Society, The Relevance of Royce, hosted by Vanderbilt University. A revised version of Auxier's paper will appear as a chapter in his forthcoming book *Time, Will and Purpose: Living Ideas in the Philosophy of Josiah Royce*.

3. Auxier, "Royce's Fictional Ontology."

4. Josiah Royce, "Kant's Relation to Modern Philosophic Progress," *Journal of Speculative Philosophy* 15 (1881): 380.

5. Josiah Royce, *The Religious Aspect of Philosophy: A Critique of the Bases of Conduct and of Faith* (1885) (Gloucester, Mass.: Peter Smith, 1965), 300.

6. Royce, *Metaphysics*, 82.

7. Ibid., 83.

8. Ibid.

9. Ibid.

10. Royce, *The Religious Aspect of Philosophy*, 302.

11. Ibid., 298.

12. Ibid.

13. Ibid., 303.

14. See ibid., 322 and 382. See Randall E. Auxier, "Josiah Royce," 2091, where he characterizes Royce's philosophic method as an idealism that "depends upon postulates and proceeds hypothetically."

15. Ibid., 300–304.

16. Ibid., 323.

17. Josiah Royce, *The Basic Writings of Josiah Royce*, ed. John J. McDermott (Chicago: University of Chicago Press, 1969), vol. I, 357.
18. Ibid.
19. Ibid.
20. Ibid., 358.
21. Ibid.
22. Ibid., 360.
23. Ibid.
24. Ibid., 362.
25. Ibid., 363.
26. See Section 5, "Reality and Experience as Correlative Conceptions," in ibid., 372–74.
27. See ibid., 368–72.
28. Ibid., 370.
29. Ibid., 371.
30. Ibid., 376.
31. Ibid., 382.
32. Ibid., 377.
33. Ibid., 379.
34. Ibid., 383.
35. I include Royce's "interpreter, the spirit of this universal community [the Community of Interpretation]" from p. 362 of *Problem of Christianity* in the list above because it is functionally equivalent to his earlier absolute (See *Problem of Christianity*, 318–19, 362, where he describes the Interpreter Spirit in terms similar to the ones used to describe the absolute in his earlier writings, e.g., "Conception of God"). This reading of Royce's *Problem of Christianity* is opposed to the contemporary Peircean interpretations of Royce's late metaphysics, which interprets Royce's late philosophy (that is, his philosophical writings of the last four or so years of his life) in terms of a non-absolutistic semiotic naturalism. Kelly A. Parker's "Josiah Royce" entry in the online *Stanford Encyclopedia of Philosophy* is a paradigmatic example of this Peircean reading of Royce. For Parker's well-written and informative encyclopedia article, last revised May 12, 2005, see http://plato.stanford.edu/archives/sum2005/entries/royce/ (accessed June 17, 2008).
36. See, for example, Josiah Royce's 1906 essay "Immortality," in *Basic Writings of Josiah Royce*, vol. II, ed. John J. McDermott (Chicago and London: University of Chicago Press, 1969), 394–95, 397. See also Royce, *Philosophy of Loyalty*, 160.
37. See Josiah Royce, *The Sources of Religious Insight* (1912) (New York: Octagon Books, 1977), 160–61.

38. Josiah Royce, "Supplemental Essay," in *Conception of God: A Philosophical Discussion Concerning the Nature of the Divine Idea as a Demonstrable Reality*, 2nd rev. and enl. ed., ed. George Holmes Howison, reprinted in *Critical Responses to Josiah Royce, 1885–1916*, ed. Randall E. Auxier (Bristol, England: Thoemmes Press, 2000), vol. I, 292.

39. For the standard division of the intellectual stages of Royce's Harvard career, see Frank M. Oppenheim, "Josiah Royce's Intellectual Development: An Hypothesis," *Idealistic Studies* 6 (January 1976): 85–102.

40. See especially Josiah Royce, "The Problem of Job," in *Studies of Good and Evil* (New York: D. Appleton, 1898), 1–28; "Immortality;" and *The Philosophy of Loyalty*.

41. See, for example, Royce, *The Problem of Christianity*, 40–41.

42. See *The Problem of Christianity*, vol. II.

43. Ibid., 61–62.

CHAPTER SIX
KING'S BELOVED COMMUNITY, ROYCE'S METAPHYSICS

1. Charles R. Johnson, "The King We Need: Teachings for a Nation in Search of Itself," *Shambhala Sun* 13.3 (January 2005): 44. Johnson describes a personalism more similar to that of Borden Parker Bowne (1847–1910) and L. Harold DeWolf (1905–1986) than the finitistic theistic personalism of Edgar Sheffield Brightman (1884–1953). While he was a graduate student, King flirted with Brightman's finistic, theistic personalism, but he reverted back to a more traditional theism with a personalist edge, of course, similar to those of DeWolf and George Davis.

2. Rufus Burrow, Jr., "Borden Parker Bowne and the Dignity of Being," *Personalist Forum* 13.1 (Spring 1997): 219; James H. Cone, *Martin and Malcolm and America: A Dream or a Nightmare?* (Maryknoll, N.Y.: Orbis Books, 2001), 30–31; Cornel West, "Martin Luther King, Jr.: Prophetic Christian as Organic Intellectual," in *Prophetic Fragments* (Grand Rapids, Mich. and Trenton, N.J.: Eerdmans/Africa World Press, 1988), 4–9.

3. Martin Luther King, Jr., *Stride Toward Freedom* (New York: Harper & Row, 1958), 100. See also Cone, *Martin and Malcolm and America*, 131–32.

4. For more on Royce as an American personalist, see *The Personalist Forum*'s special issue on the Royce–Howison "Conception of God" debate and the relevance of Royce, *Personalist Forum* 15.1 (Spring 1999) and John E. Smith's autobiographical remarks in *Personalism Revisited: Its Proponents and Critics*, ed. Thomas O. Buford and Harold H. Oliver (Amsterdam and New York: Rodopi, 2002), 255–56.

5. These divisions of King's career are inspired by Charles Johnson's novel about King's life, *Dreamer: A Novel* (New York: Simon and Schuster, 1998), and James H. Cone's *Martin and Malcolm and America*. See also Johnson, "The King We Need," 48; Cone, *Martin and Malcolm and America*, 60–61.

6. Johnson, "The King We Need," 48.

7. Cone, *Martin and Malcolm and America*, 76.

8. Ibid., 29.

9. Ibid., 76.

10. Martin Luther King, Jr., "Nonviolence: The Only Road to Freedom," in *A Testament of Hope: The Essential Writings and Speeches of Martin Luther King, Jr.*, ed. James M. Washington (San Francisco: HarperSanFrancisco, 1986), 56, and Randall E. Auxier, "Martin Luther King, Jr. and Malcolm X: Personalists on and in Community"(presented at the Personalist Discussion Group at the American Philosophical Association's Eastern Division Meeting, New York, December 27–30, 2002).

11. King, "Nonviolence," 57–58.

12. Ibid., 78.

13. Martin Luther King, Jr., *Why We Can't Wait* (1963) (New York: Signet Classic, 2000), 26–27.

14. Johnson, "The King We Need," 9.

15. Edgar Sheffield Brightman, *Moral Laws* (New York: Abingdon Press, 1933).

16. Walter G. Muelder, *Moral Law in Christian Social Ethics* (Richmond, Va.: John Knox Press, 1966).

17. Brightman, *Moral Laws*, 242. The Law of the Ideal of Personality states, "All persons ought to judge and guide all of their acts by their ideal conception (in harmony with the other Laws) of what the whole personality ought to become both individually and socially" (ibid.). The laws in Brightman's *Moral Laws* are not prescriptive, but rather regulative and suggestive (see Burrow, *Personalism*, 204). We should think of Brightman's moral laws as being moral principles (Brightman, *Moral Laws*, 242.). Brightman's personalistic ethics is, therefore, "a method for making moral judgments" (ibid.). Burrow adds, "Because [Brightman's personalistic ethics] is a system, its use requires effort and intentionality on the part of those who would use it. For in order to be most useful the moral law system must be seen in its totality, and one must be cognizant of the place and role of each law, as well as their interrelationship with each other and the entire system" (ibid.). Imagine Alfred North Whitehead constructing an organic ethical system

where each principle is not intelligible unless one also knows its relation to all the other principles in the ethical system. Then one would have Brightman's personalistic ethics.

18. Muelder, *Moral Law in Christian Social Ethics*, 119. Here is Muelder's Law of the Ideal of Community: "All persons ought to form and choose all of their ideals and values in loyalty to their ideals (in harmony with the other Laws) of what the whole community ought to become; and to participate responsibly in groups to help them similarly choose and form all their ideals and choices" (ibid.). Muelder's communitarian laws, especially his Law of the Ideal of Community, make the implicit communal dimension to Brightman's personalistic very explicit. Instead of having personalistic ethics end with a "law" regulating person-to-person ethical relationships, like Brightman does, Muelder extends personalistic ethics to the realm of human communities. King was influenced by Muelder's communitarian laws as well as Brightman's original laws (Burrow, *Personalism*, 219–20).

19. John J. Ansbro, *Martin Luther King, Jr.: The Making of a Mind*. 1982, Reprinted as *Martin Luther King, Jr.: Nonviolent Strategies and Tactics for Social Change* (Lanham, New York, and Oxford: Madison Books, 2000), 86.

20. Martin Luther King, Jr., "An Experiment of Love," in *A Testament of Hope: The Essential Writings and Speeches of Martin Luther King, Jr.*, James M. Washington, ed. (San Francisco: HarperSanFrancisco, 1986), 19.

21. Ansbro, *Martin Luther King, Jr.*, 7 and 1–36, for a relatively detailed analysis of the most significant philosophers and theologians that contributed to King's notion of love. I do not intend to highlight which parts of their conceptions of love King uses in his own notion of *agape* because such a task would take us too far away from discussing the central theses of this chapter.

22. King, *Stride Toward Freedom*, 104; King, "Experiment of Love," 19.

23. Ibid.

24. Ibid.

25. King, "Letter from Birmingham Jail," in *Why We Can't Wait*, 65.

26. See Ansbro, *Martin Luther King, Jr.*, 187–88, for a concise description of the characteristics of King's Beloved Community.

27. Ibid., 188.

28. See Cornel West, "Martin Luther King, Jr.," 5–6, and Cornel West, "Subversive Joy and Revolutionary Patience in Black Christianity," in *Prophet Fragment*, 161–65, for an enlightening discussion of African American Christian eschatology and its relation to King's Christianity.

29. Cone, *Martin and Malcolm and America*, 135.

30. Ibid., 241.

31. See Ansbro, *Martin Luther King, Jr.,* 188–97.

32. "Welcome to The Beloved Community: The Beloved Community of Martin Luther King, Jr." *The King Center* http://www.thekingcenter.org/prog/bc/index.html (accessed July 26, 2008).

33. Ibid.

34. Judith M. Green, "King's Civil Rights Act Turns Forty: Leading the Beloved Community in the Twenty-First Century" (presented at the 32nd annual conference of the Society for the Advancement of American Philosophy, Bakersfield, California, March 2005).

35. Ibid., 1.

36. Ibid., 9.

37. Ibid.

38. Johnson, "The King We Need 49.

39. See Cone, *Martin and Malcolm and America,* 232–42.

40. Cone, *Martin and Malcolm and America,* 241.

41. See Martin Luther King, Jr., "I See the Promised Land," in *A Testament of Hope: The Essential Writings and Speeches of Martin Luther King, Jr.,* ed. James M. Washington (San Francisco: HarperSanFrancisco, 1986), 279–86.

42. Martin Luther King, Jr., "Remaining Awake Through a Great Revolution," in *A Testament of Hope: The Essential Writings and Speeches of Martin Luther King, Jr.,* ed. James M. Washington (San Francisco: HarperSanFrancisco, 1986), 268–78.

43. Ibid., 270, 278.

44. See "The Beloved Community of Martin Luther King, Jr."

45. Gary L. Herstein, "The Roycean Roots of the Beloved Community," unpublished manuscript (paper presented at the Joint Group session of the Society for the Philosophy of Creativity, the Personalist Group, and the Society for the Study of Process Philosophy, 2005 American Philosophical Association Central Division Meeting, Chicago, Illinois, April 29, 2005).

46. Ibid.

47. Royce, *The Problem of Christianity,* 248–49.

48. Ibid., 261–62.

49. Ibid., 268–70.

50. Orosco, "Cosmopolitan Loyalty and the Great Global Community," 206.

51. John J. McDermott, "Classical American Philosophy: A Reflective Bequest to the Twenty-First Century," *Journal of Philosophy* 81.11 (November

1984): 672. See also Josiah Royce, "The Hope for the Great Community," in *The Basic Writings of Josiah Royce*, ed. John J. McDermott (Chicago: University of Chicago Press, 1969), vol. II, 1156–57.

52. McDermott, "Classical American Philosophy," 672.

53. See, for example, Josiah Royce, "Words of Professor Royce at the Walton Hotel at Philadelphia, 1915," in *The Basic Writings of Josiah Royce*, ed. John J. McDermott (Chicago and London: University of Chicago Press, 1969), vol. 1, 35, and John Clendenning, *The Life and Thought of Josiah Royce*, rev. and exp. ed. (Nashville: Vanderbilt University Press, 1999), 362–72, esp. 369–72.

54. King, "Nonviolence," 57–58.

CHAPTER SEVEN
COUPLING ROYCE'S TEMPORALISM WITH LEVINASIAN INSIGHTS

1. Emmanuel Levinas, *Totality and Infinity: An Essay in Exteriority*, trans. Alphonso Lingis (Pittsburgh: Duquesne University Press, 1969), 28, 62, 65–67.

2. Emmanuel Levinas, *Otherwise than Being, or Beyond Essence*, trans. Alphonso Lingis (Pittsburgh: Duquesne University Press, 1998), 183.

3. See Josiah Royce, "The Temporal and the Eternal," in *World and the Individual*, vol. II: *Nature, Man, and the Moral Order* (New York: Macmillan, 1904), 109–51; and "The Reality of the Temporal," *International Journal of Ethics* 20.3 (April 1910): 257–71 (originally presented at the American Philosophical Association, New Haven, December 29, 1909) for Royce's articulation of a Kantian sense of human temporality; see Emmanuel Levinas, "The Other, Utopia, and Justice," in *Entre Nous: On Thinking-of-the-Other*, trans. Michael B. Smith and Barbara Harshav (New York: Columbia University Press, 1998), 232, for Levinas's articulation of a similar Kantian sense of human temporality.

4. Randall Auxier was, to my knowledge, the first Royce commentator to describe Royce's ethics, and his entire philosophy, as an ethical temporalism.

5. See Royce, "Temporal and the Eternal."

6. See Royce, "Reality of the Temporal."

7. See Charles M. Sherover, *Human Experience of Time: The Development of Its Philosophic Meaning* (Evanston, Ill.: Northwestern University Press, 2001), 356–61.

8. Royce, "Temporal and the Eternal," 126–29.

9. Royce's notion of perceptual time is very similar to Ernst Cassirer's description of perceptual time in "The Human World of Space and Time," *An Essay on Man* (New Haven: Yale University Press, 1944), 50–51.

10. Ibid., 131.

11. Ibid., 130.

12. Ibid., 130–31.

13. In *Problem of Christianity*, Royce calls this purposive creative force, when in service of ethical ideals, he calls it the will to interpret.

14. Royce, "Reality of the Temporal," 134.

15. See Chapter 3 for Royce's explanation of how a human person is the result of one's present self interpreting one's past self to one's future self in *The Problem of Christianity*.

16. Royce, "Reality of the Temporal," 269.

17. Ibid., 271.

18. Edgar S. Brightman, "A Temporalist View of God," *Journal of Religion* 12 (October 1932): 545–55. Brightman misinterprets Royce's notion of the divine time span as being non-temporal on pages 554–55 of his essay. In fact, Royce affirms both the temporal nature of God and our own temporal nature in his metaphysics.

19. Royce, "Reality of the Temporal," 271.

20. See Royce, "Reality of the Temporal," 269, where Royce reminds his readers that his "view of the temporal aspect of things is part . . . of a voluntaristic idealism," namely, his idealism.

21. Royce defines the term *ethical self* in *World and the Individual*, vol. II, 245–77.

22. The "empirical Ego" is a psychological and epistemic idea that enables us to study a person as an object of scientific inquiry and empirical observation; it is an abstraction. See Josiah Royce, *Outlines of Psychology* (New York: Macmillan, 1903), 274–98; and his chapter "The Human Self," *World and the Individual*, vol. II, for more on Royce's conception of empirical Ego.

23. Royce, *World and the Individual*, vol. II, 268, quoted in Jacquelyn Ann K. Kegley, "Josiah Royce," *Pragmatism and Classical American Philosophy: Essential Readings and Interpretive Essays*, ed. John J. Stuhr, 2nd ed. (New York and Oxford: Oxford University Press, 2000), 249.

24. Royce expresses this "spiritual union of all persons" by each person acting in community, yet retaining their own individuality, quite articulately in *Philosophy of Loyalty*.

25. See, for example, Levinas, *Totality and Infinity*, 28, 62, 65–67. Unless otherwise noted, whenever "phenomenality" is mentioned in this paper, it will be used in Levinas's restricted sense of the term.

26. In Edmund Husserl, *Ideas: General Introduction to Pure Phenomenology* (1913), trans. W. R. Boyce Gibson (New York: Collier Books, 1967), Hus-

serl makes it difficult to distinguish between two phenomenological *epochés*. The first is called simply the phenomenological reduction, which puts the naturalistic attitude in abeyance, and thus enables the phenomenologist to investigate how phenomena appear to us (see, for example, 101–3). The second *epoché* is called the transcendental reduction, or less often, the transcendental-phenomenological reduction (see, for example, 103); this enables the phenomenologist to unearth the eidetic and invariant structures of the phenomena in which we co-constitute their meaning. For the remainder of this essay, whenever the phenomenological reduction is mentioned, it covers both senses of Husserl's *epoché* in this text.

27. This is not to be confused with Anthony J. Steinbock's description of Michel Henry's phenomenological reduction as an "ethical epoché." My "ethical epoché" is a form of the phenomenological reduction in which one investigates the origin of sense of ethical relationships between persons.

28. See "Preface," Levinas, *Totality and Infinity*, 21–30.

29. See, for example, ibid., 23, 227–28.

30. He announces this project in ibid., 52 and 242–45.

31. Ibid., 253.

32. Ibid., 198–201, 253.

33. The political significance of Levinas's notion of ethical time, along with his overall ethical phenomenology, is not at issue in this paper because I am interpreting Levinas's phenomenology in transcendental terms. I consider Levinas's phenomenology of the face as in *Totality and Infinity* and his "hermeneutics of subjectivity" (as Bettina Bergo calls it in *Levinas between Ethics and Politics: For the Beauty that Adorns the Earth* [Dordrecht, Boston, and London: Kluwer, 1999]), in Levinas's *Otherwise than Being* to be a phenomenological description of the condition for the possibility of genuine interpersonal conversation on the concrete level (see Martin Kavka, "Review of *Addressing Levinas*," in *Notre Dame Philosophical Review* http://ndpr.nd.edu/review.cfm?id=4781 (accessed June 18, 2008). According to such a reading of Levinas's major writings, his ethical phenomenology does not provide a specific political or social philosophy, but only "a phenomenological method that demonstrates that ethical acts and redemption are really possible" in a world governed by the logic of totality (ibid.). In other words, he offers us an alternative to the violence of history in terms of his phenomenological investigations into the conditions for the possibility of ethical phenomena—namely, the face-to-face encounter with the Other *qua* other person.

34. Edmund Husserl, "Fifth Meditation: Uncovering of the Sphere of Transcendental Being as Monadological Intersubjectivity," in *Cartesian*

Meditations: An Introduction to Phenomenology, trans. Dorion Cairns (The Hague: Martinus Nijhoff, 1977), 89–151.

35. Husserl distinguishes between these senses of the other person's alterity in *Cartesian Meditations* sects. 45, 50–54, esp. sects. 51 and 53.

36. See, for example, Levinas, *Totality and Infinity,* 28, 62, 65–67. For a concise yet thorough description of Levinas's understanding of revelation as a non-representational mode of phenomenological givenness, see Anthony J. Steinbock's "Face and Revelation: Levinas on Teaching as Way-Faring," in *Addressing Levinas,* ed. Eric Sean Nelson, Antje Kapust, and Kent Still (Evanston, Ill.: Northwestern University Press, 2005), 119–37, esp. 120–24, 134–35. See also Jean-Luc Marion, "The Voice without Name: Homage to Levinas," in *The Face of the Other and the Trace of God: Essays on the Philosophy of Emmanuel Levinas,* ed. Jeffrey Bloechl (New York: Fordham University Press, 2000), 224–42, for an account of how Levinas was the first phenomenologist to elevate the ethical appeal of the Other's face, or what Levinas calls "revelation" in *Totality and Infinity,* to the level of "a founding phenomenological act (and thus is itself not founded)" (224).

37. Indeed, Western philosophy in general has not been able to take account of the genuinely alien, that is, of the irreducible uniqueness of human persons. Instead, it has traditionally subsumed the genuinely alien and unique Other under the genus of the Same, robbing the Other of her ethical voice (see Levinas, *Totality and Infinity,* 22–23).

38. Ibid., 110–14.
39. Ibid., 129–30.
40. Ibid., 111.
41. Ibid.
42. Ibid.,115.
43. Ibid., 113.
44. Ibid., 120.
45. Ibid., 136–38.
46. Ibid., 147–48.
47. Ibid., 125.
48. Ibid.
49. Ibid., 137–39.
50. Ibid., 150–51.

51. Gabriel Marcel, *Tragic Wisdom and Beyond, including Conversations between Paul Ricoeur and Gabriel Marcel,* trans. Stephen Jolin and Peter McCormick (Evanston, Ill.: Northwestern University Press, 1973), 193.

52. Ibid., 194.

53. Ibid., 197.
54. Ibid., 199.
55. Ibid., 244–47. An excellent and amazingly idiosyncratic explication of Levinas's understanding of the face-to-face encounter between oneself and the Other is Alphonso Lingis, "Bare Humanity," in *Addressing Levinas*, ed. Eric Sean Nelson, Antje Kapust, and Kent Still (Evanston, Ill.: Northwestern University Press, 2005), 98–108, where Lingis presents several vignettes portraying how we can encounter the Other *qua* another person in Levinas's sense of "encountering the face of the Other," while resisting the all-too-human temptation of providing for her material, psychological, and spiritual needs in such a way that our conduct actually negates her alterity.
56. Ibid., 206–07.
57. See Alan Bass, "Translator's Introduction," in *Writing and Difference*, trans. Alan Bass (Chicago: University of Chicago Press, 1978), xvi, for a concise and informative explanation of the etymology of the English verb "to solicit."
58. See Ibid., 284.
59. Ibid., 284–85. See also Kavka, "Review of *Addressing Levinas*."
60. Bergo, *Levinas Between Ethics and Politics*, 295–96.
61. Levinas, *Totality and Infinity*, 284:
"Time is discontinuous; one instant does not come out of another without interruption, by an ecstasy. In continuation the instant meets its death, and resuscitates; death and resurrection constitute time. But such a formal structure presupposes the relation of the I with the Other and, at its basis, fecundity across the discontinuous which constitutes time."
62. See chaps. 11–15 of Anthony J. Steinbock, *Home and Beyond: Generative Phenomenology after Husserl* (Evanston, Ill.: Northwestern University Press, 1995) for a description of the generative phenomenological method. He provides a concise description of the generative phenomenological method on p. 260: "the task of a generative phenomenology is . . . to inquire after how historical and intersubjective structures themselves become meaningful at all." Such an inquiry involves an analysis of the intergenerational sense of social-historical institutions, cultural practices, and subject formation.
63. Levinas, *Otherwise than Being*, 9.
64. Ibid., 33–34.
65. Ibid., 162.
66. Ibid., 13.
67. Ibid., 150.

68. Husserl describes how even when the transcendental I is receptive to things sensed on a pre-cognitive level there is still a low level of sense constitution on the part of the transcendental I in such receptivity in *Edmund Husserl Collected Works,* vol. III: *Ideas Pertaining to a Pure Phenomenology and to a Phenomenological Philosophy, Second Book,* trans. Richard Rojcewicz and André Schuwer (Dordrecht: Kluwer, 1989), 225–26. For an extended phenomenological description of passive synthesis, see Part II, "Analyses Concerning Passive Synthesis: Toward a Transcendental Aesthetic," in Edmund Husserl, *Analyses Concerning Passive and Active Synthesis: Lectures on Transcendental Logic,* published as *Edmund Husserl Collected Works,* vol. IX, 39–274, trans. Anthony J. Steinbock (Dordrecht: Kluwer, 2001).

69. For a nuanced and excellent account of how the affective lure of the Other's face is analogous to the affective lure of sensed things see Leslie MacAvoy, "The Other Side of Intentionality," in *Addressing Levinas,* ed. Eric Sean Nelson, Antje Kapust, and Kent Still (Evanston, Ill.: Northwestern University Press, 2005), 109–18. MacAvoy's account of the affective lure of the Other's face is only a part of her larger examination of Levinas's notion of sensibility as the hinter side of Husserlian intentionality.

70. A transcript is in Emanuel Levinas, *Of God Who Comes to Mind,* trans. Bettina Bergo (Palo Alto, Calif.: Stanford University Press, 1998).

71. Ibid., 95.

72. Ibid., 96.

73. Emmanuel Levinas, "Diachrony and Representation," in *Time and the Other, and Additional Essays,* trans. Richard A. Cohen (Pittsburgh: Duquesne University Press, 1987), 97–120.

74. Ibid., 115.

75. For the entirety of this chapter, I mean by *alter ego* what Husserl means by it in *Cartesian Meditations: An Introduction to Phenomenology,* trans. Dorion Cairns (The Hague: Martinus Nijhoff, 1960), specifically in his *Fifth Cartesian Meditation.*

76. See, for example, Emmanuel Levinas, "Being-for-the-Other," in *Is It Righteous to Be? Interviews with Emmanuel Levinas,* ed. Jill Robbins (Palo Alto, Calif.: Stanford University Press, 2001), 118.

77. Here is an excellent explanation of what Levinas means when he mentions the "face of the Other":

"[T]he other, the concept of whom we are using at this very moment, is not invoked in a concept, but as a person. In speech, we do not just think of the interlocutor, we speak to him; we tell him the very concept we can have of him as "interlocutor in general." The one to whom I speak stands farther back, behind the concept I communicate to him. The absence of a common plane—transcendence—characterizes speech; the communicated content is, to be sure, common—or, more precisely, it becomes so through language. Invocation is prior to commonality. It is a relation with a being who, in a certain sense, is not in relation to me—or, if you like, who is in relation with me only inasmuch as he is entirely in relation to himself. He is a being beyond all attributes, which would have the effect of qualifying him, that is, of reducing him to what he has in common with other beings, of making a concept of him. It is this presence for me of a being identical to itself that I call the presence of the face. The face is the very identity of a being; it manifests itself in it in terms of itself, without a concept. The sensible presence of this chaste bit of skin with brow, nose, eyes, and mouth, is neither a sign allowing us to approach a signified, nor a mask hiding it. The sensible presence, here, de-sensibilizes itself in order to let the one who refers only to himself, the identical, break through directly." (Levinas, "The *I* and the Totality," in *Entre Nous*, 32–33.)

78. An excellent and amazingly idiosyncratic explication of Levinas's understanding of the face-to-face encounter between oneself and the Other is Alphonso Lingis, "Bare Humanity," in *Addressing Levinas*, ed. Eric Sean Nelson, Antje Kapust, and Kent Still (Evanston, Ill.: Northwestern University Press, 2005), 98–108, where Lingis presents several vignettes portraying how we can encounter the Other *qua* another person in Levinas's sense of "encountering the face of the Other," while resisting the all-too-human temptation of providing for her material, psychological, and spiritual needs in such a way that our conduct actually negates her alterity.

79. For a concise yet thorough description of Levinas's understanding of the "face of the Other" as a revelatory mode of phenomenological givenness, see Anthony J. Steinbock, "Face and Revelation: Levinas on Teaching as Way-Faring," in *Addressing Levinas*, ed. Eric Sean Nelson, Antje Kapust, and Kent Still (Evanston, Ill.: Northwestern University Press, 2005), 119–37, esp. 120–24, 134–35. One could interpret Steinbock as saying that the face of the Other gives herself to us in the mode of an unequivocally *moral* revelation and that we should ideally welcome her as a gift of revelation.

CLOSING REMARKS

1. The following encounter with Josiah Royce's anti-essentialist racism began in the spring of 2005. More specially, it began as a series of conversations with Tommy J. Curry. He convinced me to see Royce's views on race and racism through the lens of Derrick Bell, Jr.'s racial realism thesis. To-

gether we examined how Royce's racial anti-essentialism is still a racist position. Curry's examination of this issue led him to write a paper entitled "Mr. Charlie and the Horror of Shadows: The Limitation of Loyalty and the Negro Problem in Royce." He also presented a paper criticizing Royce's anti-essentialist yet racist position entitled "The Lil' White Man Who Could: Josiah Royce's Cultural Perpetuation of White Supremacy" (presented at Joint Session of the Josiah Royce Society and the Personalist Discussion Group, 2008 American Philosophical Association Central Division Meeting, Chicago, April 19, 2008). My examination of this issue led me to write the concluding pages of this book.

2. See Jacquelyn Ann K. Kegley, "Is a Coherent Racial Identity Essential to Genuine Individuals and Communities? Josiah Royce on Race," *Journal of Speculative Philosophy* 19.3 (2005): 216–28.

3. See, for example, ibid., 216–19.

4. Josiah Royce, "Race Questions and Prejudices," in *Race Questions, Provincialism, and Other American Problems*, reprinted in *The Basic Writings of Josiah Royce* (1908) (Chicago: University of Chicago Press, 1969), 1105.

5. Ibid., 1107–10; see also Elizabeth Duquette, "Embodying Community, Disembodying Race: Josiah Royce on 'Race Questions and Prejudices,'" *American Literary History* 16.1 (2004): 51–52.

6. Lawrence Bobo, James R. Kluegel, and Ryan A. Smith, "Laissez-Faire Racism: The Crystallization of a Kinder, Gentler, Antiblack Ideology," in *Racial Attitudes in the 1990s: Continuity and Change*, eds. Steven A. Tuch and Jack K. Martin (Westport, Conn.: Praeger, 1997), 16.

7. Ibid.

8. Ibid.

9. See Lewis R. Gordon, *An Introduction to Africana Philosophy* (Cambridge: Cambridge University Press, 2008), 3–4.

10. Royce, "Race Questions and Prejudices," 1098–99.

Bibliography

Anderson, C. Alan, and Deborah G. Whitehouse. *New Thought: A Practical American Spirituality*. New York: Crossroad Publishing Company, 1995.

Ansbro, John J. *Martin Luther King, Jr.: The Making of a Mind*. 1982. Reprinted as *Martin Luther King, Jr.: Nonviolent Strategies and Tactics for Social Change*. Lanham, New York, and Oxford: Madison Books, 2000.

Auxier, Randall E. "Editor's Introduction." In *Critical Responses to Josiah Royce, 1885–1916*. Vol. I. *The Conception of God*. Ed. Randall E. Auxier. Bristol, England: Thoemmes Press, 2000. v–x.

———."Howison's and Hocking's Critique of Royce." *Personalist Forum* 15.1 (Spring 1999): 59–83.

———. "Josiah Royce." In *Dictionary of Modern American Philosophers*. Vol. IV. Ed. John R. Shook. Bristol, England: Thoemmes Press, 2005. 2089–96.

———. "Martin Luther King, Jr. and Malcolm X: Personalists on and in Community." Presented at the Personalist Discussion Group at the American Philosophical Association's Eastern Division Meeting, New York, December 27–30, 2002.

———. "Royce's Fictional Ontology," in *The Relevance of Royce*. Ed. Kelly Parker and Jason M. Bell. New York: Fordham University Press, forthcoming.

———. *Time, Will and Purpose: Living Ideas in the Philosophy of Josiah Royce*. Chicago: Open Court Press, forthcoming.

Auxier, Randall E., ed. Critical Responses to Josiah Royce, 1885–1916, Vol. I. *The Conception of God*. Vol. 3. *Papers in Honor of Josiah Royce on His Sixtieth Birthday*. Bristol, England: Thoemmes Press, 2000.

Bass, Alan. "Translator's Introduction." In *Writing and Difference*. Chicago: University of Chicago Press, 1978. ix–xx.

Bergo, Bettina. *Levinas between Ethics and Politics: For the Beauty that Adorns the Earth*. Dordrecht: Kluwer, 1999.

Bernasconi, Robert. "The Alterity of the Stranger and the Experience of the Alien." In *The Face of the Other and the Trace of God: Essays on the Philosophy of Emmanuel Levinas*. Ed. Jeffrey Bloechl. New York: Fordham University Press, 2000. 62–89.

Bertocci, Peter A., and Richard M. Millard. *Personality and the Good: Psychological and Ethical Perspectives*. New York: David McKay, 1963.

Brightman, Edgar S. *Moral Laws*. New York: The Abingdon Press, 1933.

———. "Temporalist View of God." *Journal of Religion* 12 (October 1932): 544–55.

Buford, Thomas O. "What We Are About." *Personalist Forum* 1.1 (1985): 1–4. Available online at http://www.siu.edu/~tpf/Volume%201%20Web%20Files/Volume%201_1%20Editors%20Introduction.pdf (accessed July 25, 2008).

Burrow, Rufus, Jr. "Borden Parker Bowne and the Dignity of Being." *Personalist Forum* 13.1 (Spring 1997): 13–30.

———. *Personalism: A Critical Introduction*. St. Louis, Missouri: Chalice Press, 1999.

Cassirer, Ernest. "Human World of Space and Time," *An Essay on Man*. New Haven: Yale University Press, 1944. 42–55.

Cesarz, Gary. "Howison's Pluralistic Idealism: A Fifth Conception of Being?" *Personalist Forum* 15.1 (Spring 1999): 28–44.

———. "A World of Difference: The Royce-Howison Debate on the Conception of God." *Personalist Forum* 15.1 (Spring 1999): 84–128.

Chanter, Tina. *Time, Death, and the Feminine: Levinas with Heidegger*. Palo Alto, Calif.: Stanford University Press, 2001.

Clendenning, John, ed. *Letters of Josiah Royce*. Chicago: University of Chicago Press, 1970.

———. *Life and Thought of Josiah Royce*. Revised and expanded edition. Nashville: Vanderbilt University Press, 1999.

Cohen, Richard A. *Elevations: The Height of the Good in Rosenzweig and Levinas*. Chicago and London: University of Chicago Press, 1994.

Costello, Harry T. *Josiah Royce's Seminar, 1913–1914*. New Brunswick: Rutgers University Press, 1963.

Cotton, James H. *Royce on the Human Self*. Cambridge, Mass.: Harvard University Press, 1954.

Cowan, Rosemary. *Cornel West: The Politics of Redemption*. Malden, Mass.: Polity Press, 2003.

Curry, Tommy J. "The Lil' White Man Who Could: Josiah Royce's Cultural Perpetuation of White Supremacy." Presented at Joint Session of the Josiah Royce Society and the Personalist Discussion Group, 2008 American Philosophical Association Central Division Meeting, Chicago, Illinois, April 19, 2008.

———. "Mr. Charlie and the Horror of Shadows: The Limitation of Loyalty and the Negro Problem in Royce." Unpublished manuscript.

Dewey, John. *A Common Faith*. Reprinted in *Later Works of John Dewey*. Ed. Jo Ann Boydston. Carbondale, Ill.: Southern Illinois University Press, 1989. Vol. IX, 1–60.

———. *Experience and Nature*. Reprinted in *Later Works of John Dewey*. Ed. Jo Ann Boydston. Carbondale, Ill.: Southern Illinois University Press, 1988. Vol. I, 3–326.

Duquette, Elizabeth. "Embodying Community, Disembodying Race: Josiah Royce on 'Race Questions and Prejudices.'" *American Literary History* 16.1 (2004): 29–57.

Emerson, Ralph Waldo. "Self-Reliance." *Selections from Ralph Waldo Emerson: An Organic Anthology*. Ed. Stephen E. Whicher. Boston: Houghton Mifflin Company, 1960. 147–68.

Flewelling, Ralph Tyler. "George Holmes Howison: Prophet of Freedom." *Personalist* 38.1 (Winter 1957): 5–19.

Flower, Elizabeth and Murray G. Murphey, eds. *A History of Philosophy in America*. New York: G. P. Putnam's Sons, 1977. Vol. II.

Garchar, Kim. "Sin, Sorrow, and Suffering: A Graceful Response to the Deeper Tragedies of Life." Presentation at the 34th annual Society for the Advancement of American Philosophy. March 10, 2007.

Gordon, Lewis R. *An Introduction to Africana Philosophy*. Cambridge: Cambridge University Press, 2008.

Green, Judith M. "King's Civil Rights Act Turns Forty: Leading the Beloved Community in the Twenty-First Century." Presented at the 32nd annual conference of the Society for the Advancement of American Philosophy, Bakersfield, California, March 2005.

Harris, Errol E. *Restitution of Metaphysics*. Amherst, N.Y.: Humanity Books, 2000.

Herstein, Gary L. "The Roycean Roots of the Beloved Community." Presented at the Joint Group session of the Society for the Philosophy of Creativity, the Personalist Group, and the Society for the Study of Process Philosophy, 2005 American Philosophical Association Central Division Meeting, Chicago, Illinois, April 29, 2005.

Howison, George Holmes. "The City of God and the True God as Its Head." *The Conception of God: A Philosophical Discussion Concerning the Nature of the Divine Idea as a Demonstrable Reality.* 1897. Ed. George Holmes Howison. Reprinted in *Critical Responses to Josiah Royce, 1885–1916.* Ed. Randall E. Auxier. Bristol, England: Thoemmes Press, 2000. Vol. I, 81–132.

———. "Josiah Royce: The Significance of His Work in Philosophy." In *Critical Responses to Josiah Royce, 1885–1916.* Ed. Randall E. Auxier. Bristol, England: Thoemmes Press, 2000. Vol. III, 3–16.

———. *The Limits of Evolution, and Other Essays Illustrating the Metaphysical Theory of Personal Idealism.* 2nd revised and enlarged ed. New York: Macmillan, 1904.

Husserl, Edmund. *Cartesian Meditations: An Introduction to Phenomenology.* Trans. Dorion Cairns. The Hague: Martinus Nijhoff, 1960.

———. *Edmund Husserl Collected Works.* Vol. III. *Ideas Pertaining to a Pure Phenomenology and to a Phenomenological Philosophy, Second Book: Studies in the Phenomenology of Constitution.* Trans. Richard Rojcewicz and André Schuwer. Dordrecht: Kluwer, 1989 [1912–28].

———. *Edmund Husserl Collected Works.* Vol. IV. *On the Phenomenology of the Consciousness of Internal Time (1893–1917).* Trans. John Barnett Brough. Dordrecht: Kluwer, 1991.

———. *Edmund Husserl Collected Works.* Vol. IX. *Analyses Concerning Passive and Active Synthesis: Lectures on Transcendental Logic.* Trans. Anthony J. Steinbock. Dordrecht: Kluwer, 2001 [1920–26].

———. *Ideas: General Introduction to Pure Phenomenology.* Trans. W. R. Boyce Gibson. New York: Collier Books, 1967 [1913, 1931].

———. *On the Phenomenology of the Consciousness of Internal Time (1893–1917).* Trans. and ed. John Barnett Brough. Dordrecht: Kluwer, 1991.

James, William. "Stream of Thought." *Principles of Psychology.* 1890. New York: Henry Holt and Company, 1927. 224–90. Reprinted in *The Writings of William James.* Ed. John J. McDermott. Chicago and London: University of Chicago Press, 1977. 21–74.

Jarvis, Edward. *The Conception of God in the Late Royce.* The Hague: Nijhoff, 1975.

Johnson, Charles. *Dreamer: A Novel.* New York: Simon and Schuster, 1998.

Kant, Immanuel. *Fundamental Principles of the Metaphysics of Morals.* Trans. T. K. Abbott. Amherst, N.Y.: Prometheus Books, 1988.

Kavka, Martin. "Review of *Addressing Levinas.*" In *Notre Dame Philosophical Review* http://ndpr.nd.edu/review.cfm?id=4781 (accessed June 18, 2008).

Kearney, Richard. *The God Who May Be: A Hermeneutics of Religion.* Bloomington and Indianapolis: Indiana University Press, 2001.

Kegley, Jacquelyn Ann K. "Grace, the Moral Gap, and Royce's Beloved Community." *Journal of Speculative Philosophy* 18.3 (2004): 171–83.

———. "Is a Coherent Racial Identity Essential to Genuine Individuals and Communities? Josiah Royce on Race." *Journal of Speculative Philosophy* 19.3 (2005): 216–28.

———. "Josiah Royce: Anticipator of European Existentialism and Phenomenology," In *Doctrine and Experience: Essays in American Philosophy*. Ed. Vincent G. Potter. New York: Fordham University Press, 1988. 174–89.

———. "Royce and Husserl: Some Parallels and Foods for Thought." *Charles S. Peirce Society* 14.3 (Summer 1978): 184–99.

King, Martin Luther, Jr., *Stride Toward Freedom*. New York: Harper & Row, 1958.

———. *Why We Can't Wait*. New York: Signet Classic, 2000 [1963].

Kohak, Erazim. "Personalism: Toward a Philosophical Delineation." *Personalist Forum* 13.1 (Spring 1997): 3–11.

Kuklick, Bruce. *A History of Philosophy in America 1720–2000*. Oxford: Clarendon Press, 2001.

———. *Josiah Royce's Intellectual Biography*. Indianapolis: Bobbs, 1972.

———. *The Rise of American Philosophy*. New Haven: Yale University Press, 1977.

Leahy, D. G. "The Person as Absolute Particular." Presentation at Seventh International Conference on Persons. August 2003. Unpublished manuscript.

Leibniz, G. W. *Discourse on Metaphysics*. 1686. In *Philosophical Essays*. Trans. R. Ariew and D. Garber. Indianapolis: Hackett Publishing Company, 1989. Reprinted in *Modern Philosophy: An Anthology of Primary Sources*. Ed. Roger Ariew and Eric Watkins. Indianapolis: Hackett Publishing Company, 1998. 184–207.

———. *Principles of Philosophy or the Monadology* (1714). In *Philosophical Essays*. Trans. R. Ariew and D. Garber. Indianapolis: Hackett Publishing Company, 1989. Reprinted in *Modern Philosophy: An Anthology of Primary Sources*. Ed. Roger Ariew and Eric Watkins. Indianapolis: Hackett Publishing Company, 1998. 235–43.

Levinas, Emmanuel. "Diachrony and Representation." In *Time and the Other, and Additional Essays*. Trans. Richard A. Cohen. Pittsburgh, Pa.: Duquesne University Press, 1987 [1982]. 97–120.

———. *Discovering Existence with Husserl*. Trans. and ed. Richard A. Cohen and Michael B. Smith. Evanston, Ill.: Northwestern University Press, 1998.

———. *Entre Nous: On Thinking-of-the-Other*. Trans. Michael B. Smith and Barbara Harshav. New York: Columbia University Press, 1998 [1991].

———. *Of God Who Comes to Mind.* Trans. Bettina Bergo. Palo Alto, Calif.: Stanford University Press, 1998 [1986].

———. *Is It Righteous to Be? Interviews with Emmanuel Levinas.* Ed. Jill Robbins. Palo Alto, Calif.: Stanford University Press, 2001.

———. *Otherwise Than Being, or Beyond Essence.* Trans. Alphonso Lingis. Pittsburgh: Duquesne University Press, 1998 [1974, 1981].

———. *Totality and Infinity: An Essay in Exteriority.* Trans. Alphonso Lingis. Pittsburgh: Duquesne University Press, 1969 [1961].

Lingis, Alphonso. "Bare Humanity." In *Addressing Levinas.* Ed. Eric Sean Nelson, Antje Kapust, and Kent Still. Evanston, Ill.: Northwestern University Press, 2005. 98–108.

Loewenberg, J. "Editor's Introduction." In *Fugitive Essays.* Essay Index Reprint Series. Freeport, N.Y.: Books for Libraries Press, Inc., 1968 [1920]. 3–37.

MacAvoy, Leslie. "The Other Side of Intentionality." In *Addressing Levinas.* Ed. Eric Sean Nelson, Antje Kapust, and Kent Still. Evanston, Ill.: Northwestern University Press, 2005. 109–18.

McLachlan, James. "George Holmes Howison: The Conception of God Debate and the Beginnings of Personal Idealism." *Personalist Forum* 11.1 (Spring 1995): 1–16.

———. "George Holmes Howison's 'The City of God and the True God as Its Head': The Royce–Howison Debate over the Idealist Conception of God." *Personalist Forum* 15.1 (Spring 1999): 5–27.

Marcel, Gabriel. *Royce's Metaphysics.* Trans. Virginia Ringer and Gordon Ringer. Chicago: Henry Regnery Company, 1956.

———. *Tragic Wisdom and Beyond, Including Conversations between Paul Ricoeur and Gabriel Marcel.* Trans. Stephen Jolin and Peter McCormick. Evanston, Ill.: Northwestern University Press, 1973 [1968].

Marion, Jean-Luc. "The Voice without Name: Homage to Levinas." In *The Face of the Other and the Trace of God: Essays on the Philosophy of Emmanuel Levinas.* Ed. Jeffrey Bloechl. New York: Fordham University Press, 2000. 224–42.

Oppenheim, Frank M., Sr. "High Points in Josiah Royce's Intellectual Development." *Metaphysics.* Ed. William Ernest Hocking, Richard Hocking and Frank Oppenheim. Albany: State University of New York Press, 1998. xv–xvi.

———. *Reverence for the Relations of Life: Re-imagining Pragmatism via Josiah Royce's Interactions with Peirce, James, and Dewey.* Notre Dame, Ind.: University of Notre Dame Press, 2005.

———. *Royce's Mature Ethics*. Notre Dame, Indiana: University of Notre Dame Press, 1993.

———. *Royce's Mature Philosophy of Religion*. Notre Dame, Indiana: University of Notre Dame Press, 1987.

———. *Royce's Voyage Down Under*. Lexington: University Press of Kentucky, 1980.

Orosco, José-Antonio. "Cosmopolitan Loyalty and the Great Global Community: Royce's Globalization." *Journal of Speculative Philosophy* 17.3 (2003): 204–15.

Parker, Kelly A. "Josiah Royce." *Stanford Encyclopedia of Philosophy* (Summer 2005 Edition). Ed. Edward N. Zalta http://plato.stanford.edu/archives/sum2005/entries/royce/.

Peperzak, Adriann T., Simon Critchley, and Robert Bernasconi, eds. *Emmanuel Levinas: Basic Philosophical Writings*. Bloomington and Indianapolis: Indiana University Press, 1996.

Powell, Thomas F. *Josiah Royce*. New York: Washington Square Press, 1967.

Punzo, Vincent C. "Royce on the Problem of Individuality." Dissertation. St. Louis University, 1963.

Rodemeyer, Lanei. "Developments in the Theory of Time-Consciousness: An Analysis of Protention." *The New Husserl: A Critical Reader*. Ed. Donn Welton. Bloomington, Ind.: Indiana University Press, 2003. 125–54.

Royce, Josiah. *The Basic Writings of Josiah Royce*. Vols. I–II. Ed. John J. McDermott. Chicago: University of Chicago Press, 1969.

———. "The Conception of God." *The Conception of God: A Philosophical Discussion Concerning the Nature of the Divine Idea as a Demonstrable Reality*. 1897. Ed. George Holmes Howison. Reprinted in *Critical Responses to Josiah Royce, 1885–1916*, Vol. I. *The Conception of God*. Ed. Randall E. Auxier. Bristol, England: Thoemmes Press, 2000. 3–50.

———. *Fugitive Essays*. Essay Index Reprint Series. Ed. J. Loewenberg. Freeport, N.Y.: Books for Libraries Press, Inc., 1968 [1920].

———. *Josiah Royce's Late Writings: A Collection of Unpublished and Scattered Works*. Vols. I–II. Ed. Frank M. Oppenheim, S.J. Bristol, England: Thoemmes Press, 2001.

———. *Metaphysics*. Ed. William Ernest Hocking, Richard Hocking, and Frank Oppenheim. Albany, N.Y.: State University of New York Press, 1998.

———. *Outlines of Psychology*. New York: Macmillan, 1903.

———. *The Philosophy of Loyalty*. Nashville: Vanderbilt University Press, 1995 [1908].

———. *The Problem of Christianity*. Washington, D.C.: Catholic University of America Press, 2001 [1913].

———. "Reality of the Temporal." *International Journal of Ethics* 20.3 (April 1910): 257–71.

———. *The Religious Aspect of Philosophy*. New York: Harper, 1958 [1885].

———. *The Sources of Religious Insight*. New York: Octagon Books, 1977 [1912].

———. *Spirit of Modern Philosophy*. Boston: Houghton Mifflin, 1896.

———. *Studies of Good and Evil*. New York: D. Appleton and Co., 1898.

———. *William James and Other Essays on the Philosophy of Life*. Essay Index Reprint Series. Freeport, N.Y.: Books for Libraries Press, 1969.

———. *The World and the Individual, Vol. I: Four Historical Conceptions of Being*. New York: Macmillan, 1899.

———. *The World and the Individual, Vol. II: Nature, Man, and the Moral Order*. New York and London: Macmillan, 1904 [1901].

Sherover, Charles M. *From Kant and Royce to Heidegger: Essays in Modern Philosophy*. Ed. Gregory R. Johnson. Washington, D.C.: Catholic University of America Press, 2003.

———. *Human Experience of Time: The Development of Its Philosophic Meaning*. Evanston, Illinois: Northwestern University Press, 2001 [1975].

Sia, Santiago. *God in Process Thought*. Dordrecht: Martinus Nijhoff, 1985.

Smith, John E. "Creativity in Royce's Philosophical Idealism." In *Contemporary Studies in Philosophical Idealism*. Ed. John Howie and Thomas O. Buford. Cape Cod, Mass.: Claude Stark & Company, 1975. 197–215.

———. *Royce's Social Infinite*. New York: The Liberal Arts Press, 1950.

Steinbock, Anthony J. "Face and Revelation: Levinas on Teaching as Way-Faring." In *Addressing Levinas*. Ed. Eric Sean Nelson, Antje Kapust, and Kent Still. Evanston, Ill.: Northwestern University Press, 2005. 119–37.

———. *Home and Beyond: Generative Phenomenology after Husserl*. Evanston, Ill.: Northwestern University Press, 1995.

Trotter, Griffin. *The Loyal Physician: Roycean Ethics and the Practice of Medicine*. Nashville: Vanderbilt University Press, 1997.

———. "Royce, Community and Ethnicity." *Transactions of the Charles S. Peirce Society*, 30.2 (1994): 231–69.

Tuch, Steven A. and Jack K. Martin, eds. *Racial Attitudes in the 1990s: Continuity and Change*. Westport, Conn.: Praeger, 1997.

Tunstall, Dwayne A. "Concerning the God That Is Only a Concept: A Marcellian Critique of Royce's God." *Transactions of the Charles S. Peirce Society: A Quarterly Journal in American Philosophy* 42.3 (Summer 2006): 394–416.

———. "Josiah Royce's Personalism." Master's thesis. Southern Illinois University Carbondale, May 2004.

———. "Royce and King on *Agape* and the Beloved Community." Presented at the Joint Group Session of the Society for the Philosophy of Creativity, the Personalist Discussion Group, and the Society for the Study of Process Philosophy, 2005 American Philosophical Association Meeting, Central Division, Chicago, Illinois, April 29, 2005.

Tyman, Stephen. "Problem of Evil in the Royce-Howison Debate." *Personalist Forum* 13.2 (Fall 1997): 107–121.

———. "Royce and the Destiny of Idealism." *Personalist Forum* 15.1 (Spring 1999): 45–58.

"Welcome to the Beloved Community: The Beloved Community of Martin Luther King, Jr." *The King Center* http://www.thekingcenter.org/prog/bc/index.html (accessed July 26, 2008).

Werkmeister, W. H. *A History of Philosophical Ideas in America.* New York: Ronald Press Co., 1949.

West, Cornel. "Pragmatism and the Sense of the Tragic." Reprinted in *The Cornel West Reader.* New York: Basic Civitas Books, 1999. 174–82.

Wicks, Robert. "Arthur Schopenhauer." *Stanford Encyclopedia of Philosophy.* http://plato.stanford.edu/entries/schopenhauer/ (accessed July 19, 2008).

Wieman, Henry Nelson. *Wrestle of Religion with Truth.* New York: Macmillan, 1928.

Zondervan KJV Study Bible. Grand Rapids, Michigan: Zondervan, 2002.

Index

A Common Faith (Dewey), 3
A History of Philosophical Ideas in America (Werkmeister), 28–29
A History of Philosophy in America (Murphey), 10
A Study of Religion (Martineau), 20
Absolute
   as actual experience, 36
   as agapic love, 72
   as completed actuality, 36
   Hegelian Absolute, 10
      pluralistic monism and, 71–72
   as individual, 10
   individuality and, 71
   as living logos, 9
   non-causality of as Ideal, 147n–48n
   possibilities and, 36, 143n
   as preserver of all particularities, 10
   proving existence to non–Judeo-Christian, 25
   removal from ontological vocabulary, 49
absolute, eternality, 93
Absolute Experience, 18–19, 22–24, 138n–39n
absolute idealism, Howison's abandonment, 14
Absolute particular, 18
Absolute Thought, 138n–39n
   The Religious Aspect of Philosophy and, 9
absolutist metaphysics of Royce's early philosophical career, 9–10

absolutistic idealism, 137n
abstract infinite, Parker, Theodore, 20
acting ethically, respecting other persons and, 80
activistic epistemology, 74
actual, use of word, 34
actuality, 34, 37
African Americans, racism against, 133
agape
   Brightman, Edgar S., 99–100
   King, Martin Luther Jr., 5, 100
   loyalty and, 104
   Mueller, Walter G., 99–100
   nonviolence and, 99
   Royce and, 104
   tough love, 43
   will to interpret and, 104
agapic love
   eternal Ideal, 41
   St. Paul and, 53–54
   will to interpret and, 52, 105–6
agnosticism, solipsism and, 142n–43n
All-Knower, 17
All-Servant, 55
Alter Ego, 20
Ansbro, John J., 102
appreciation, description and, 30
argument for existence of God, "The Conception of God," 19
atheists' loyalty to God, 143n
attempt to solve problem of evil, "The Problem of Job" as, 31
autonomous selves, God as Absolute Experience and, 23–24

Auxier, Randall E., 140n
  on Howison, George Holmes, 11
  Modern Dictionary of American Philosophers, 86
  Royce's cessation of idealism, 12
awareness of dependence on other persons and non-personal beings to know ourselves and world, 19

being, use of word, real and, 35
beings
  minded and non-minded, 39
  as ongoing temporal process, 39
Beloved Community, 1
  actualization, 106
  approximation of, 12
  communal persons and, 69
  divine allure of, 3
  divine person and, 56
  emergence of, our participation in, 65
  God as ideal of, 74
  King, Martin Luther Jr., 5, 101–3, 106, 155n–56n
  let life be guided by, 54
  The Problem of Christianity, 104
  universe as personal cosmos responding to, 78–79
  will to interpret as real phenomenon, 53
  will to interpret as spirit of, 52
Bergo, Bettina, 122
Berkeley Philosophical Union debate, 15
Bertocci, Peter A., 73
Beyond, sensitivity to, 21
Bobo, Lawrence, 133
Body of Christ, 2, 53
Boston personalism, 13
  panentheistic personalism and, 77
  philosophical viability, 77–78
  Royce and, 73–74
  Royce's personalism and, 67–68
Bowne, Borden Parker, 70, 140n
Brightman, Edgar S., 3, 73
  consistency, 44
  Law of the Ideal of Personality, 99
  Moral Laws, 99, 159n–60n

Burrow, Rufus Jr., 138n
  idealistic personalism and, 80
  Royce's idealism as personalistic absolutism, 71

chefs and knives, 58
City of God, 13
  metaphysics of community and, 62–63
civility, struggle for, 48
Clendenning, John, 30, 140n
communal persons, 57, 68–69
community
  all-servant and, 55
  anticipation of future, 52
  building, will to interpret and, 52
  as communal person, 57
  hope, 52
  identity and, 56–57
  loyalty and, 43–44
  memory, 52
  metaphysics of, Pauline Christianity and, 53
  non-community, 52
  Paul's description of Body of Christ, 53
  self-representative selves, Absolute and, 53
  society, 52
  spirit of Universal Community, 53
  universe as, respect and, 78
Community of Interpretation, 18, 104
  Interpreter Spirit, 12
community of interpreters, 20
concentric metaphysics, 37
conception of God, 63
  criticism, Royce's response to, 29
  Kantian transcendental argumentation and, 89–90
  philosophical, 90
  Royce's argument for, 16
concepts, as objects of knowledge, 89
conceptual present, 112
concrete experiences, 38
Cone, James, 101–2
consciousness, communal persons, 69
Cotton, James H., 137n

creator, relationship between creator and creature, 145n
creator of world, God as, 74
Critical Responses to Josiah Royce (Auxier), 11–12
cult of the dead, 152n

Darwinian evolutionary theory, 63
dead, cult of, 152n
dependence on other selves, 61
description, appreciation and, 30
Dewey, John, 3, 78, 138n
"Diachrony and Representation" (Levinas), 126
Discourse on Metaphysics (Leibniz), 31
divine
   temporality, 154n
   totality of the Real and, 49
divine grace, communal persons and, 69
divine living self, 20
divine person, 55–56
divine will, 65
dualistic epistemology, 74
dualistic mind-object relation, 74
duty, 59–60
   as members of community, 63

eating to live, 118
egoism, Same and, 118
embodiedness, human experience and, 60
Emerson, Ralph Waldo, 44
enjoyment, 118–19
epistemology, 74–76
error
   phenomenalists and, 16–17
   The Religious Aspect of Philosophy, 16
   the unknowable and, 17
eternal, 114
the Eternal
   the Absolute, 49
   as observer, 47
eternity, 1
   Royce's definition, 49
   The Sources of Religious Insight and, 49

ethical, Same and, 118
ethical and panentheistic personalism, 77
ethical futurity, messianic time and, 125
ethical personalism, Howison, 73
ethical self, 61
ethical temporality, 123, 125
ethical time, 116–17, 164n
   self-temporalization and, 123
ethics of responsibility, 58–59
evil, metaphysics and, 31
evolution, emergence of personal organisms and, 78
evolutionary love, 2
experience, 20
   absolute life and, 38
   concrete, 38
   lived, as starting-point for inquiries, 62
   metaphysical realism and, 38
   natural beings, 20
   ontological locus of experience, 39
   as origin for knowledge, 38
   Royce's reverence for, 38
experiential warrant for believing in God's existence, 25
experientialism, panexperientalism, 92
Extension Course on Ethics, 31, 56–62
"Extension Course on Ethics," 4
exteriority of things and persons, 120
external reality, 88

fecundity and paternity, Levinasian *epoché* and, 122
felt experiences, 151n
fictional ontology, Royce's advancing, 5
Fifth Cartesian Meditation (Husserl), 117
finite beings, limits, 18
Flewelling, Ralph Tyler, 13
future
   reality of, 113
   responsibility for the Other, 126
future self, 113, 114

Gandhi, Mohandas, 96
generative phenomenological method, 166n

German influences on Royce's thought, 26
God
    as Absolute Being, 31–32
    as Absolute Experience, autonomous selves and, 23–24
    actualizable ideals and, 49
    as agapic love, 41
    athiests' loyalty to, 143n
    as co-experiencer of the world, 32
    conception of, 63
    as conceptual expression of ethico-religious postulate, 92–93
    creation, 36–37
    creator of world, 74
    existence of
        experiences, 22
        experiential warrant for believing in, 25
    as fellow sufferer, 32
    hypothetical, 94
    as ideal, 41
    as immanent in the world, 32
    as logical principle, 50
    as noumenal existence, 50
    omnipotence, 41
    as ontological preserver of temporality, 74
    as personal God, 32
    as Personal Self, 22
    personalism and, 72
    as philosophic postulate, 93
    possibilities and, 37
    as preserver of interrelated system of finite beings, 22
    relationship between actual experience and possible experiences, 21
    The Religious Aspect of Philosophy, 94
    Royce, 94
    as spirit who experiences what we experience, 32
    sufferings, 32
    temporality, 38–39, 93
    Temporality and, 72
    "The Conception of God," 94
    triumph over evil, "The Problem of Job" on, 32–33
    as triumphant, moral God, 33
    as weaver, 39
    as World-ground, 74
God *qua* philosophical concept, 91
God's existence, 19, 70
grace, 1
Green, Judith, 102

Harris, William Torrey, 13, 14, 15
Hegel, G. W. F., 11
Hegelian Absolute, 10
    pluralistic monism and, 71–72
Hegelian pantheism, "Conception of God" debate, 13
Hegelianism, Howison on, 13–14
Herstein, Gary, 104
highly evolved organisms with self-referential cognition, 60
history, totality and, 116
Holy Spirit, will to interpret and, 105
Howison, George Holmes, 3
    abandonment of Hegelianism, 141n
    Absolute, 24–25
    American personal idealism, 13–14
    attack on Possibility of Error argument, 26
    attack on Royce's version of absolute idealism, 14–15
    conception of God, 63
    criticism of Hegelianism of his era, 13
    on eternity, 64
    ethical personalism, 73
    existential choice, 25–26
    as founder of philosophical position, 14
    God as Kantian philosophical deity, 64
    Hegelianism, abandonment of, 14
    idealism, compared to Royce's idealism, 62–66
    influence on Royce, 11
    irritation at Royce for displacement at Harvard, 140n
    Kant and, 25–26
    letters to William Torrey Harris, 13, 14, 15
    The Limits of Evolution, 13, 14

misinterpretation of Royce's conception of God, 32
personal idealism, 4, 65, 140n
   Boston personalism and, 13
   initial presentation, 14
   persons as personality of God, 14
   philosophical viability, 77–78
   pluralistic philosphy, 14
   Royce's idealism and, 12–13
personalism and, 140n
pluralistic idealism, personal idealism, 13–14
plurality as facsimiles of Transcendent Self, 13
plurality as manifestations of Absolute, 13
response to "The Conception of God," 23–24
Royce's absolute idealism, 13
Royce's conception of God and individuality, 24
Royce's idea of autonomous selves, 24
as Royce's philosophical foil, 11–12
Royce's response to criticism
   of absolute idealism, 38
   of conception of God, 29
teleological personalism, 73
"The City of God and the True God as Its Head," 23–24
The World and the Individual and, 38
Howisonian personalism, 65
human experience, embodiedness and, 60
human ignorance, 91
human persons
   according to Royce, 56
   as communal self, 57
   as individual self, 57
   as ethical selves, 115
   living apart from others, 60–61
   as manifestations of divine life, 33
   tripartite analysis, 61
human temporality, Other and, 115–16
Husserl, Edmund
   ethical temporality, 123
   Fifth Cartesian Meditation, 117
   living present, 119
   other persons, 117
   phenomenology, 115–16
hypothetical propositions, 92

I, 123–24
"I am, because we are . . ." quote, 71
Ideal, Beloved Community, divine will as, 65
ideal experience, reality and, 91–92
idealism, 12–13
   Howison's personal idealism and, 12–13
   late, 12
      plurality of persons, 13
      unity of persons, 13
   pantheism and, 70
   as personalistic absolutism, 71
   as proto-process philosophy, 70
   Royce's compared to Howison's, 62–66
   shift in, 12
idealistic personalism, 79–80
identity
   community and, 56–57
   life-plan and, 56, 115
ignorance, human, 91
illeity, 124–25
immanent order, 42
immemorial past, messianic time and, 125
immortality, 152n
indefinite present, 119
individual persons
   personality of, 69
   realness of, 68
individuality, Absolute and, 71
Ineffable Mystery, 23
Infinite Person, divine will as, 65
Infinite Self, 60
intelligibility of the now intended object, 119
intending noema, 119
intentionality, 119, 123–24
interpersonal world, participation in, 122

interpretation of reality
  as community of persons, 72
  as impersonal universe, 72
  stubbed-toe example, 75–76
interpretation of self, 57–58, 72
Interpreter Spirit, 12, 71–72, 139n
  will to interpret and, 104–5
interpreter-spirit of Universal Community, 53–54
interpreting our environment, 54

James, William, 11
Jamesian psychology, 60
Jim Crow racism, 133, 134
John-Thomas argument, 17–18
Johnson, Charles R.: King, Martin Luther Jr. and, 96

Kant, Emmanuel, 25–26, 86
"Kant's Relation to Modern Philosophic Progress," 86–87
Kelsey, George, 97
kinesthetic passive syntheses, 125
King, Martin Luther Jr., 96–97
  agape, 5
  Beloved Community, 5, 101–3, 106–7
  Bowne, Borden Parker and, 157n
  Brightman, Edgar S. and, 157n
  criticism of United States, 103
  DeWolf, L. Harold and, 157n
  doctrine of nonviolence, 97–99
  idealistic personalism and, 80
  "Letter from Birmingham Jail," 100–101
  metaphysics of community and, 107
  nonviolence, 5
  personalism, similarity to Royce's, 155n–56n
  public philosophy, 97
  Vietnam War opposition, 103
Kluegel, James, 133
Kohak, Erazim, 67–68
Kuklick, Bruce, 10

laissez-faire racism, 133
late idealism as proto-process philosophy, 70

"Law of the Ideal of Personality" (Brightman), 100
Leahy, D. G., 18
LeConte, Joseph, 11, 15
Leibniz, G. W., 11, 31
Leibnizian monads, 60
"Letter from Birmingham Jail" (King), 100–101
levels of personhood, 68–69
Levinas, Emmanuel, 5
  critique of Royce's temporalism, 126–28
  epoché, 116
  ethical time, 116–17
  face of the Other, 167n–68n
  Marcel's being, 120
  human temporality, Other and, 115–16
  messianic future, 125
  Other, face-to-face encounter, 117–18
  Otherwise than Being, 111, 123–26
  revelation, 117
  Royce's egological view of temporality, 127
  Totality and Infinity, 111, 116
  University of Leyden, 125
life guided by Beloved Community, 54
life-plan, 40
  identity and, 56, 115
literature on Royce's philosophy, 138n
lived experience, 62, 151n
living apart from others, 60–61
living present, 119, 124
Lockean empiricism, 39
Loewenberg, Jacob, 35
logic in Royce's philosophizing, 138n
logos, Absolute as, 9
Logos-Spirit, 2, 55
Lotze, Rudolf, 87–88
love, evolutionary, 2
loyalty
  agape and, 104
  author's anecdote, 46–47
  community and, 43–44
  to loyalty, 43–47
  loyalty to, 1

Marcel, Gabriel
  being, Levinas' face of the Other, 120
  Royce's Metaphysics, the unknowable, 17
  on Royce's philosophical thought as of 1899, 33–35
  Tragic Wisdom and Beyond, 120
masculine pronoun usage, 139n
Mays, Benjamin E., 97
McLachlan, James, 16
  Howison's abandonment of Hegelianism, 141n
  Howison's claim to be Hegelian, 13
messianic future, immemorial past and, 125
messianic time, immemorial past and, 125
metaphysical realism, experience and, 38
metaphysical schema, 37
metaphysical self, 61
metaphysics, 71
  evil and, 31
metaphysics of community, 2
  delineation of, 10
  Howison's City of God and, 62–63
  intermediate stage, 38
  King, Martin Luther Jr. and, 107
  Pauline Christianity and, 53
  The Philosophy of Loyalty, 47
metaphysics of interpretation, 139n
Meulder, Walter, 80
Mezes, Sidney, 15
minded beings, 39, 147n
  Beloved Community, 53
  identity of, 56
  intelligibility of universe, 54
Mitsein, 60
modal logic, 143n–44n
Modern Dictionary of American Philosophers (Auxier), 86
modes of an Infinite Self, 60
Monadology (Leibniz), 31
moral experience, 59–60
Moral Law in Christian Social Ethics (Muelder), 99
Moral Laws (Brightman), 99, 159n–60n

moral standing, struggle for, 48
Muelder, Walter G., 99, 160n
Münsterberg, Hugo, 11
Murphey, Murray G., 10
mutual interdependence between Absolute and finite individuals, 10

naturalistic humanism, 78
Nature, purposes, 42
Niebuhr, Reinhold, 98
noema, intending, 119
noetic-noematic structure of Husserlian intentionality, 117
non-minded beings, 39, 147n
nonviolence
  agapic love, 99
  King, Martin Luther Jr., 5, 97–99

omnipotence of God, 41
omniscient being, 90–91
ontological argument for God's existence, relational form, 70
ontological distinction between finite beings and Absolute, 39–40
ontological locus of experience, 39
ontological preserver of temporality, God as, 74
ontological vocabulary, 34
Oppenheim, Fr. Frank M., 2, 137n
  analysis of Royce's tripartite analysis of personhood, 61
  early Royce, 93–94
  on Kuklick's interpretation of Royce, 10–11
  Logos-Spirit, 55
  Royce's ethics of responsibility, 58–59
  Royce's periods, 138n
  Royce's Voyage Down Under, 26–27
originary source, illeity as, 124
Other
  as absolutely other, 121
  elusiveness, 120
  face of, 117
    Levinas, 167n–68n
    lure of, 125
    visceral quality of encounter, 125
  face-to-face encounter, 117–18, 121–22

future as responsibility for, 126
I, time and, 124
non-phenomenal speech of, 121
recession into the past, 125
temporality and, 115–16, 121
Thou shall not murder, 121
transcendence, 121
Otherwise than Being, Or Beyond Essence (Levinas), 111
ethical temporality, 123–26

panentheism, 32, 145n–46n
panentheistic personalism, 76–77
panexperientialism, 92
Parker, Theodore, 20
Passivity, 125
past
present experience and, 26
reality of, 113
past self, 113
Pauline Christianity, 2
agapic love, 53–54
metaphysics of community and, 53
Paul's description of Body of Christ, 53
Peirce, Charles S.
evolutionary love, 2
influence on Royce, 11
semeiotics, ethics of responsibility, 58–59
people
dependence on other people, 71
as irreducibly distinct embodied being, 71
perceptual time, specious present, 112
perpetual fellow-sufferer, divine will as, 65
Perry, Ralph Barton, 78
personal beings, relating to world, 72
personal organisms, evolution and, 78
personalism
1 John 4:13 and, 71
ethical and panentheistic, 77
God and, 72
Howisonian personalism, 65
Howison's personal idealism, 13, 65
King, Martin Luther Jr., 155n–56n
Kohak, Erazim, 67–68

panentheistic, 76–77
The Personalist Forum, 67
Royce's, personalistic absolutism, 70
personalist, Royce as, 65, 153n
personalistic absolutism, 70–71
personhood, levels, 68–69
persons, *causa sui*, 74
phenomenalists, error, 16–17
phenomenological reduction, 164n
phenomenological self, 61
phenomenology, proto-phenomenology, 111–12
phenomenology of concept formation, 88–89
philosophical conception of God, 90
verifiability, 92
philosophical knowledge, 89
philosophical postulates, God as, 93
philosophical theology of Royce, 22–23
Plato, 11
pluralistic monism, Hegelian Absolute and, 71–72
possibilities
Absolute and, 36
imaginable, 37
as potentialities, 37, 143n, 147n
possibilities *qua* possibilities, 37, 147n
Absolute and, 143n
Possibility of Error argument, 16, 17–19
Howison's attack on, 26
postulates, 87–89
potentiality, 37
present experience, past and, 26
present self, 113, 114
proto-phenomenology, 111–12
Punzo, Vincent C., 140n
purposes
Nature, 42
selves, 41
purposive purposefulness of Nature, 148n
purposiveness, 41

racism, 132–35
Randall, John Herman Jr., 78
rational animals, 60
Rauschenbusch, Walter, 96

INDEX

real, use of word, 147n
the Real
  interpreting, 54
  totality of, 146n
reality
  as divine Whole, 9–10
  ideal experience and, 91–92
  as matrix of interrelated beings, 26
  use of word, being and, 35
realness of communal and individual persons, 68
reductio ad absurdum arguments, 38
relating to world as personal beings, 72
relational form of ontological argument for God's existence, 70
relational proto-process philosophy, 30
relationships, 71
religiosity of Royce's thought, 3
revelation, Levinas, 117
rope analogy for structure of communal person, 57
Royce, Josiah
  as personalist, 153n
  agape and, 104
  as American personalist, 3
  Boston personalists and, 73–74
  conception of God, 63
  divine, temporality, 154n
  empiricists and, 38
  German influences, 26
  Germany and, 107, 148n–49n
  Howison, response to criticism of conception of God, 29
  idealism, 154n
    compared to Howison's idealism, 62–66
    as personalistic absolutism, 71
  Kant and, 25–26
  King, Martin Luther Jr. and, 5
  late idealism, as proto-process philosophy, 70
  literature on philosophy, 138n
  logic and, 138n
  Peirce, Charles S. and, 143n
  periods, Oppenheim and, 138n
  personalism
    American personalist tradition and, 4–5
    Boston personalists and, 67–68
    Burrow, Rufus and, 5
    Howison, George Holmes and, 4
  as personalist, 65
  philosophical theology of, 22–23
  as poet-philosopher, 1
  postulates, dissatisfaction with, 87
  as process philosopher, 144n
  quotes, 1
  The Religious Aspect of Philosophy, 87
  Schopenhauer and, 143n
  temporalism, 5
    Levinas and, 126–30
  voluntarism, 144n
  war stance and, 107–8
  writing to William James, 29
  "Royce's Fictional Ontology," 86
  Royce's Mature Ethics (Oppenheim), 59
  Royce's Metaphysics (Marcel), the unknowable, 17
  Royce's philosophy, ineffability and, 1
  Royce's Voyage Down Under (Oppenheim), 26–27
Ryder, John, 78

Same
  egoism and, 118
  ethical and, 118
samurai and sword, 58
Santayana, George, 78
Schopenhauer, Arthur, 11
Scripture
  1 John 4:13, personalism and, 71
self, divine living self, 20
self-knowledge, as interpretive act performed on us by ourselves, 18
selves
  dependence on, 61
  purposes, 41
sense impressions, 88
Seventh International Conference on Persons, 18
Sherover, Charles, 111
"Simplify your Christology," 54
Smith, John, 139n

Smith, Ryan, 133
society, Royce's definition, 52
Society for the Advancement of American Philosophy, 3
solipsism, agnosticism and, 142n–43n
specious present, 112
Spinoza, Benedict de, 11
Spirit of Beloved Community, 139n
  will to interpret as, 52
spiritual union, 45–46, 147n
spontaneous acts, 155n
stubbed-toe example, 75–76
Studies of Good and Evil, 29
sufferings, God's sufferings, 32
Supplementary Essay, 18, 41

teleological personalism, Howison, 73
temporal awareness, 112–13
temporal density of beings, 38–39
temporal events, totality, 114
temporal existence of the I, 123–24
temporal reality of God, 39
temporal structure of human persons, 113
temporal world, as sequence of novel and individual events, 114
temporalism, 5–6
  Levinas' critique of Royce, 126–28
  Royce's, 111
  Levinasian insights and, 128–30
temporality
  of God, 93
  divine, 154n
  God and, 38–39, 72
  of the I, intentionality and, 123–24
  Other and, 115–16
  will and, 114
The Aspect of Philosophy (Royce), proof for God's reality, 87
"The City of God and the True God as Its Head" (Howison), 23–24
"The Conception of God," 4, 10, 90
  argument for existence of God, 19
  disagreement between Royce and Howison, 16
  relational ontological argument, 20

the Eternal, *The Sources of Religious Thought*, 49
The Human Experience of TIme (Sherover), 111
"The Law of the Ideal of Community" (Muelder), 100
The Law of the Ideal of Personality, 159n
The Limits of Evolution (Howison), 13
"The Person as Absolute Particular," 18
The Personalist Forum
  Conception of God, 16
  personalism and, 67
The Philosophy of Loyalty, 1, 4, 43–50
The Problem of Christianity, 1, 4
  Beloved Community, 104
  comentators on, 10
  "Community of Interpretation," 18
  community of interpreters, 20
  Peirce's influence on Royce, 11
  as reply to Howison, 52–56
"The Problem of Job," 2, 4, 29–33
"The Reality of the Temporal," 6
The Religious Aspect of Philosophy, 4, 15, 29, 87
  Absolute Thought and, 9
  error, 16
  God's existence, 90
  phenomenology of concept formation, 88
  "Possibility of Error," John-Thomas argument, 17, 18
  postulates, 87
The Sources of Religious Insight, 1
  commentators on, 10
  eternity, 49
The Sources of Religious Thought, 48–49
The Spirit of Modern Philosophy, 20, 30
"The Temporal and the Eternal," 111, 113
The World and the Individual
  Howison and, 38
  "Supplementary Essay," 18
third-person masculine pronoun usage, 139n
Thurman, Howard, 97
time
  death and, 166n

I and Other, 124
  of intentionality, 123–24
  modalities of, 124
time-consciousness, 112–13
timelessness, eternal and, 114
total self, 35
totality
  conversion of alien to familiar, 117
  history and, 116
  Levinas, dangers of, 117
Totality and Infinity (Levinas), 111, 116
totality of temporal events, 114
totum simul of reality, 19
tough love, 43
Tragic Wisdom and Beyond (Marcel), 120
transcendence
  meaning, 121
  Other, 121
transcendence of brute physicality, 79
Transcendent Self, 13
transcendental-phenomenological reduction, 164n
transcendental reduction, 164n
triadic interpretative epistemology, 74–76

Unconscious Reality, 23
Union debate, 1895
  attack from Howison, 30
  Werkmeister, W. H., and, 28
unitas multiplex, 73
unity of persons, City of God and, 13
Universal Community, 104
  interpreter-spirit, 53–54
Universal Substance, 23

universe
  as community, respect and, 78
  as cosmic accident, 78
  as personal cosmos responding to Beloved Community, 78–79
unknowability, 17
the unknowable, 17

Wallace, George, 99
Werkmeister, W. H., 3, 28
West, Cornel, 80
what experiences us in our totality, 21
whole self, 35
will, 113–14
will to interpret
  agape and, 104
  as agapic love, 52
  agapic love and, 105–6
  communities of hope, 52
  communities of memory, 52
  community building and, 52
  Holy Spirit and, 105
  Interpreter Spirit and, 104–5
  as real phenomenon in Beloved Community, 53
  as spirit of Beloved Community, 52
Williams, A. D., 97
Wissenschaft, 15
world as creation of mind, 21
world as personal one, 12
World-ground, God as, 74
World Spirit, 10

Zeitgeist, 101
Zondervan KJV Study Bible, 137n

AMERICAN PHILOSOPHY SERIES
Douglas R. Anderson and Jude Jones, series editors

Kenneth Laine Ketner, ed., *Peirce and Contemporary Thought: Philosophical Inquiries.*

Max H. Fisch, ed., *Classic American Philosophers: Peirce, James, Royce, Santayana, Dewey, Whitehead,* second edition. Introduction by Nathan Houser.

John E. Smith, *Experience and God,* second edition.

Vincent G. Potter, *Peirce's Philosophical Perspectives.* Ed. by Vincent Colapietro.

Richard E. Hart and Douglas R. Anderson, eds., *Philosophy in Experience: American Philosophy in Transition.*

Vincent G. Potter, *Charles S. Peirce: On Norms and Ideals,* second edition. Introduction by Stanley M. Harrison.

Vincent M. Colapietro, ed., *Reason, Experience, and God: John E. Smith in Dialogue.* Introduction by Merold Westphal.

Robert J. O'Connell, S.J., *William James on the Courage to Believe,* second edition.

Elizabeth M. Kraus, *The Metaphysics of Experience: A Companion to Whitehead's "Process and Reality,"* second edition. Introduction by Robert C. Neville.

Kenneth Westphal, ed., *Pragmatism, Reason, and Norms: A Realistic Assessment—Essays in Critical Appreciation of Frederick L. Will.*

Beth J. Singer, *Pragmatism, Rights, and Democracy.*

Eugene Fontinell, *Self, God, and Immorality: A Jamesian Investigation.*

Roger Ward, *Conversion in American Philosophy: Exploring the Practice of Transformation.*

Michael Epperson, *Quantum Mechanics and the Philosophy of Alfred North Whitehead.*

Kory Sorrell, *Representative Practices: Peirce, Pragmatism, and Feminist Epistemology.*

Naoko Saito, *The Gleam of Light: Moral Perfectionism and Education in Dewey and Emerson.*

Josiah Royce, *The Basic Writings of Josiah Royce.*

Douglas R. Anderson, *Philosophy Americana: Making Philosophy at Home in American Culture.*

James Campbell and Richard E. Hart, eds., *Experience as Philosophy: On the World of John J. McDermott.*

John J. McDermott, *The Drama of Possibility: Experience as Philosophy of Culture.* Edited by Douglas R. Anderson.

Larry A. Hickman, *Pragmatism as Post-Postmodernism: Lessons from John Dewey.*